1 - 6 - 49

New York City

THE FOLD-OUT MAP on the opposite page and the smaller maps which introduce the first three sections of this book are tools as well as guides. They show the areas investigated by the book's divisions, correlate material within the sections and help to show the relationship of each section to the volume as a whole. The outline map at the top of this page places New York City's five boroughs.

On the large map opposite, solid lines divide the borough of Manhattan into three arbitrary sections. Detailed maps of these first three lettered sections introduce those sections in the book. The Section A map is on page 36; Section B, page 120; Section C, page 234. The sectional maps contain circled numbers locating main picture stories, and the first page of each story carries the number to locate it on the sectional map. This function for Section D—which covers the boroughs other than Manhattan, and the city's environs—is performed by the fold-out map on the opposite page, where the location of Section D's stories are indicated by numerals.

Railroad, airline, bus and highway facilities into the city, as well as transportation within the city, are described in the story beginning on page 363. On page 362 is a map of the subway network. Highway distances to the city are indicated on a map on page 385. Main roads used by autos and buses are shown on the fold-out map. For further detail, standard road maps should be consulted.

This book, devoted to the American metropolis and world capital, attempts to report, in words and pictures, on as many specific places and attractions as possible. Therefore no concerted attempt has been made to interpret the geographical or cultural growth of the city from its beginnings.

New York City

← ══════ UNFOLD FOR MAP OF NEW YORK CITY ══════════════

a LOOK
PICTURE
BOOK

LOOK AT AMERICA

New York City

BY THE EDITORS OF LOOK

IN COLLABORATION WITH FREDERICK LEWIS ALLEN

A HANDBOOK IN PICTURES, MAPS AND TEXT FOR THE

VACATIONIST, THE TRAVELER AND THE STAY-AT-HOME

ONE OF THE LOOK AT AMERICA REGIONAL VOLUMES

HOUGHTON MIFFLIN COMPANY BOSTON

THE RIVERSIDE PRESS   CAMBRIDGE

Contents

New York City

FREDERICK LEWIS ALLEN *brings a background of 25 years of living and working in the New York area to his essay on the skyscrapered city. Born in Boston on July 5, 1890, he was on the staffs of the* Atlantic Monthly *and* Century *magazines before joining* Harper's Magazine *in 1923, of which he has been editor since 1941. He has written three books,* Only Yesterday, The Lords of Creation *and* Since Yesterday; *and of the three volumes of pictures and text on which he has collaborated with his wife, Agnes Rogers,* The American Procession, Metropolis *and* I Remember Distinctly, *the second dealt wholly with New York City.*

The Editors of LOOK

INTRODUCTION

New York City

BY FREDERICK LEWIS ALLEN

STANDING the other day on a New York City street-corner two blocks away from the gray-and-silver shaft of the Empire State Building, I saw, far above me, what looked like a tiny insect clinging to the building's side. It was a window-cleaner at work some sixty stories above the street.

I had just come by subway from the Wall Street district of the city, where the noon-hour pedestrians swarmed in virtual twilight, as at the bottom of an Alpine gorge, along narrow streets between vertical cliffs of masonry hundreds of feet high.

The subway train which I had taken from Wall Street to midtown Manhattan had been making a run of some fifteen miles in all, from Brooklyn to the northern Bronx, tunneling under two rivers on its way; and at whatever station one might have left it, from the beginning of its long journey to the end, one would have emerged into a city scene—paved streets, apartment houses, shops, neon signs. One could have changed trains midway and traveled another seven or eight miles at right angles to one's former course, and again have come out into the sunlight to find oneself still in New York City—more paved streets, more apartment houses, more shops.

The insect-like window-cleaner, the lunch-going clerks in their dim gorge, the trains that whirl mile after mile under the earth but still cannot shake themselves free of the city—all are mere hints of the scale of this metropolis, a scale so mighty that few visitors to the city, and for that matter few residents, ever fully comprehend it. Greater London is more populous, to be sure, with over eight and a half million people as against less than eight million for New York; but one must also take into account New York's satellite cities—such as Newark and Jersey City—to say nothing of its clusters of crowded suburbs to the west and north and east, all of which bring the population of the region within forty miles of City Hall to something like eleven million. And population totals are not the whole story. For the peculiar physical location of New York City at the ocean's edge, on land broken by harbors and bays and rivers, has made it perforce a place of crowding skyscrapers and mighty bridges and tunnels—triumph after triumph over limitations and obstructions imposed by nature. Whether or not the most populous, this is certainly the most dynamic and spectacular nucleus of mankind on earth.

Let us look at the dimensions of New York in another way. We all know that it began as a small settlement at the southern tip of the twelve-and-a-half-mile-long island of Manhattan. This settlement grew slowly northward as the tide creeps up a beach, flinging block after block of new dwellings into the fields and woods of the upper island, and slowly washing before it, wave by wave, the retail shopping center, the entertainment center, the center of fashion. Fifty years ago the heart of midtown Manhattan was not far from Twenty-third Street and Fifth Avenue, where the Flatiron Building was soon to become an object of awe and delight to sightseers. Forty years ago the center of gravity had moved up to Thirty-fourth Street and Fifth Avenue, where stood the great brick-and-sandstone mass of the old Waldorf-Astoria Hotel, on the site of the present Empire State Building. Thirty years ago it had moved still farther, to Forty-second Street

10

Springtime, Park Avenue

and Fifth Avenue, where the new marble Public Library looked down upon the "busiest corner in the world." Today I think most people would agree that the heart of midtown Manhattan is in the neighborhood of Fiftieth Street and Fifth Avenue, where St. Patrick's Cathedral faces the towers of Rockefeller Center. This process of northward growth is quite familiar to visitors to the city; but there has been a sequel which they may not have fully grasped.

Across the East River, in the early days, had stood the village —which became the city—of Brooklyn, and various other villages such as Williamsburg, Jamaica, and Flushing. Across the Harlem River had been other settlements such as industrial Mott Haven and the township of Morrisania. Not only did the tide of humanity, overrunning Manhattan, surge across the rivers, swell these growing towns, and merge them into continuous communities, but about thirty years ago the island of Manhattan, already built up from end to end, began to lose population to them. For it was increasingly becoming an enormous business district, with less and less room for people to live. Its resident population actually shrank, while the resident populations of the dormitory boroughs of Brooklyn and Queens and the Bronx grew with a new rapidity. The result is that today Brooklyn, with a population of over two and a half millions, has more people than Philadelphia; while Queens and the Bronx, with nearly a million and a half apiece, *each* has more people than either Cleveland or St. Louis.

Of the visitors who converge upon New York from other parts of the country at the rate of scores of thousands every day, few ever set foot in these outlying boroughs. To most of them, perhaps, the Bronx is a nondescript area through which the New York Central and New Haven trains roar in cuttings on their way to Grand Central; Brooklyn is a name which suggests to them the Dodgers, and Brooklyn jokes, and a touchy pride, and possibly a waterfront of docks and warehouses glimpsed from a ferry; Queens is another nondescript area through which the airline limousines hum on their way from La Guardia Airport. That

12

George Washington Bridge

each of these boroughs is in dimensions and population a major city of the United States may escape comprehension. Yet only if one sees the boroughs, and the suburbs beyond them, as vital parts of the great metropolitan constellation, pouring more than two million workers into Manhattan daily by subway and commuter train, and nourishing simultaneously their own innumerable semi-independent neighborhoods, can one grasp the complexity of the New York pattern. To think of downtown and midtown Manhattan—the region of huge office-buildings and hotels and theaters and department stores and glittering show windows—as "New York" is to look at the mountain peak without seeing the massive structure of slopes and ridges and buttresses which supports it and is one with it.

The diversity of New York has become a legend. In the excellent WPA guidebook you will read that it is "the world's most populous Italian city outside of Italy . . . the world's third Irish city . . . the world's Negro metropolis . . . the greatest city of the Jews." It has room, too, for thousands of people of French origin, other thousands of German origin, and still others who preserve in some degree the customs of China, of Syria, of Greece, of Russia—the list could be extended almost indefinitely. I half believe the story of the foreigner who settled on upper Fifth Avenue, just above 110th Street, and made it his business to learn the language of the country, only to discover after a while that what he was learning was Spanish.

Nor have foreigners been the only people whom the magnet of New York has drawn from afar. For it is a new frontier for American talent, too, pulling in young brains and ambition from every part of the United States. For generations now the process has been almost continuous, and there seems to be no withstanding it. I remember meeting a young man of gifts and energy in a Western town some years ago, and thinking how well the town could use qualities like his, only to be buttonholed by an elder friend of his who said to me, "I wish you would talk to Joe Smith. There's really no future for him here. He ought to go to

14

St. Luke's Place, Greenwich Village

New York." The city is full of Joe Smiths—and Mary Smiths, too.

But even more impressive than the diversity of New York is the fact that it can absorb such millions of people and set so few boundaries between them.

Nothing so successfully resists generalization as the social structure of a community, the pattern of attractions and snobberies and emulations which determines who shall be flattered to receive an invitation to whose house. But I think it is safe to say that once New York had a Society with a capital S, though it was always a shifting group; but that the time has long since passed when even the diligence of society editors, or of the organizers of débutante parties, or of the compilers of the *Social Register,* has been able to persuade more than a few people that the concept is not two-thirds fiction. For in a city so huge, the number of prosperous and well-bred and agreeable people is so great as to defeat any arbiter. Bankers, lawyers, manufacturers, merchants, brokers, publishers, advertising people, radio people, theatrical people, journalists, professors, and their families move along endlessly shifting and interlacing paths of acquaintance and friendship. You can live twenty years in Manhattan, go to an old friend's apartment for dinner, and find that half the guests are delightful people whom you might expect to have known but whom you've never laid eyes on before—and the next week. and the week after you'll repeat the experience. The fact is that the community has grown to a point where it is a community no longer but a complex of networks of personal associations too intricate to trace.

If such a city constantly attracts newcomers, as New York does, these newcomers find themselves on their own, divorced from their backgrounds, as would hardly be possible anywhere else. If they have ability and personality, few people will bother to take much trouble to find out where or what they came from. This fact makes New York a paradise for able and ambitious people who can acquire the metropolitan patina (and for four-flushers, too—witness the remarkable career of the ex-convict,

16

Philip Musica, who changed his appearance, changed his name to F. Donald Coster, and became the respected head of a reputable firm, unquestioned in his new role until he was found to have been doctoring the company books).

Look at this well-groomed man coming down Madison Avenue: you can't tell by looking at him whether his parents voyaged by steerage from Naples, or scrabbled on a New England farm, or were factory hands in Dayton, or had a mansion at Newport, and it won't matter much anyhow to most of the people who will determine either his business or his social destiny. Look at this photogenic young woman. If she can get her hands on some money, and has an adroit clothes sense and an alert ear, pretty soon you would be hard put to it to decide whether her forebears were Park Avenue or First Avenue; New York is full of Elizas who need no Professor Higgins to instruct them in the accepted accents and manners of the town.

It is not simply the lure of money which attracts talent to New York; it is the sense that the city is a free-for-all where anybody with a gift, and push, and luck—especially luck—may be able to arrive, if not at wealth or fame, at least at recognition hard to come by elsewhere.

To be sure, the fences are not all down. The color line, though blurred increasingly, remains; Harlem is almost like a separate city. But the other racial or foreign quarters are far less clearly defined, now that the days of mass immigration are over and the second and third generations of Europeans are merging themselves into the general scheme. A careful student of Manhattan neighborhoods can point out to you German restaurants and movie houses and shops in East Eighty-sixth Street; but this Yorkville neighborhood and the people in it look much like other neighborhoods and people, and scattered through it you will find New Yorkers whose origins are Irish or Puerto Rican or Cape Cod. Chinatown and Little Italy and the Ghetto of the Lower East Side merge into one another almost indistinguishably. So fluid is apartment-house living, and so vague and complex the

18

social pattern, that one can tell less about a person from his home address than in almost any other city. The Upper West Side is predominantly Jewish, as are certain parts of Brooklyn and Queens and the Bronx; wealth and fashion tend to gravitate to the East Sixties and Seventies, between Fifth Avenue and Lexington, or to the Beekman Place or Sutton Place or East End Avenue areas; and Greenwich Village still attracts a good many artists and people of Bohemian tastes. But every one of these generalizations is subject to endless exceptions. And there is nothing more characteristic of New York than the cluster of shops—say on Third Avenue—which serve not only the upper-bracket banker's family who live in the eighteen-story apartment house, but also the Greek florist's family who live in the walk-up tenement two doors away. In this melting pot the melting proceeds in a hundred scattered and indeterminate centers.

Politics has hastened the process rather than hindered it. For each party, with a thoughtful eye to the Irish Catholic vote, the Italian vote, the Jewish vote, the Negro vote, and so on, tries to present at each election a slate on which all these elements are represented. Thus the political lines tend to be drawn across the lines of family origin. Not that New York is any utopia of tolerance: certain businesses tend to be reserved chiefly for Gentiles, while Jews predominate in the garment trade and the amusement business; and there is a tendency among Gentile lawyers and doctors to resist the infiltration of Jews into these professions. Yet on the whole the fences which divide men are few and low, and the traffic that flows around them, unfenced, is heavy.

What makes New York? What sustains it?

Well, for one thing it is a great seaport—by far the greatest in the United States. It is also a great financial center, whose Stock Exchange is the pre-eminent market for securities, whose leading banks are the biggest in the country, whose financial influence is felt by corporations the country over (though since 1933 this has been partly overshadowed by that of the government in Washington). New York is the leading textile center

20

Coney Island

of the country and the chief seat of the great garment industry, and has a considerable printing industry. It has a very lively and varied wholesale trade, and more important still is the volume of its retail trade: New York is the chief mart for luxuries, the show window of the nation. It specializes in giving visitors a good time at its theaters, restaurants, night clubs, sporting arenas, and therefore has a very flourishing hotel industry. It is the chief publishing, advertising, and radio center. With Columbia and New York University and the various city colleges, it is something of an educational center. . . .

But as we proceed with our list, you may notice that most of the functions we are including are not functions inherent in the special location of New York, and that few of them directly involve manufacturing. Most of them are functions which the city exercises because it is a seat of financial and business authority, an intellectual center, a cultural center, a place to which gravitate people and money: because, in short, New York is, in almost everything but government, the capital of the United States. It attracts new businesses because it already has assembled the key enterprises and key people with whom they must be in touch.

The economists tell us that in the most primitive societies, the chief economic activity is agricultural; that in a somewhat more advanced society, manufacturing becomes important; but that after the standard of living reaches a certain point, the chief economic activity is in the "service industries"—which include transportation, merchandising, and all the functions of government, finance, health, information, education, personal service, etc. Any city tends to be a nucleus of the service occupations; New York is pre-eminently so. Not only that, but probably a larger proportion of its inhabitants work in offices, engaged in transactions on paper, than anywhere else in America. Thomas Hornsby Ferril, a resident of Denver, once expressed his satisfaction at having just seen several hundred sheep on a hillside; on the Eastern seaboard, he said, there are many people who deal in sheep without ever looking at a living animal. The East, he contended,

22

The Cloisters and Hudson River

tends to trade in abstractions—data on a sheet of paper. As to New York, this is strikingly true. New York is a place where to hundreds of people, General Motors is not a collection of roaring factories, but the letters GM on a ticker tape; where men give their life to the cotton business without seeing a growing plant; where men render, on paper, judgments on facts presented to them on paper by people who ascertained these facts by studying findings prepared for them on paper. For this is GHQ, where the battlefront is a map on the wall and the battle is a series of written orders and written reports.

There is no more urbanized community, probably, in the whole world—no place where life is carried on to such a degree by pushing buttons, turning taps, telephoning orders, writing out orders for services; where so many people spend so much of their time under artificial light; where exercise involves such long expeditions to such artificial and (for most sports) expensive playgrounds; or where so many people look sleek and pale-faced. Although a great many New Yorkers hanker after the outdoors and a simpler life, and some manage to maintain at considerable expense a place in the country—in Connecticut or New Jersey or on Long Island—where they can more or less elaborately pursue what they think of as simplicity, few of them would really want to live long away from the nerve-centers of our civilization. And they feel in their bones that the nerve-centers are here, in the metropolis.

Not that many of them can spare the energy, even if they have the money, to go in for any such round of gaiety as the visiting couple from Kansas City engage in when they check in at the Biltmore or the St. Regis—much less to emulate the visiting buyer from Dallas to whom New York is one part business and three parts terrific spree. (I have heard it suggested that one reason why New York is regarded with distrust if not dislike in other parts of the country is that many a child has been warned at his mother's knee that New York is the wicked place where Daddy acquires a hangover and a blonde.) Most New Yorkers

24

Washington Square Arch

work pretty hard; many work under such strain that only stomach ulcers will slow them up. But they relish the sense of being where important things are going on, where the best shows and the most interesting people are to be seen, where power resides.

Bang-whang-whang, goes the drum, *tootle-te-tootle* the fife. Oh, a day in the city square, there is no such pleasure in life!

* * *

There is much in New York that is ugly. A good deal of the city was built of brownstone in the latter half of the nineteenth century, and if there is anything more hideous than a long block of chocolate-colored houses with high front steps and curlicued moldings and massive, overhanging cast-iron cornices, I don't know what it is. (If you should be perverse enough to want to see this phenomenon at its worst, I recommend a look at some of the West Side blocks between Central Park West and Broadway in the Seventies and Eighties.) There are dismal, run-down areas that progress has overleaped and left to fester in ramshackle neglect. In general, the heedlessness with which New York until recently has thrown away the possible public benefits of its superb location has been a disgrace. What will a future generation say of a community which had 578 miles of riverfront and harborfront to enjoy, and not only thoroughly polluted the water but cluttered the shores with warehouses, coal yards, freight yards, and railroad tracks?

Nor have more recent years been altogether kind to New York's appearance. The subway, while fast and safe, has become steadily more dingy and more barbarously overcrowded. The Grand Concourse in the Bronx, a potentially noble avenue miles in length, offers a remarkable exhibit of mediocre monotony, and in certain parts of Queens the higgledy-piggledy assemblage of buildings of all possible types of contractor architecture, and the space-wasting design of houselots, offer textbook demonstrations of the total absence of any sort of rational over-all planning.

There are noteworthy inconveniences, too. One of them was perpetrated a long time ago, when the city fathers laid out the

basic design for the whole middle and upper part of Manhattan. Believing that most of the traffic north and south would be by river, they built a great many cross streets east and west to afford easy access to the water, and only a few avenues, wide apart, running north and south. The result was an inordinate number of sunless rooms on the north side of houses, and also an inordinate amount of traffic congestion.

Considering the age of the city, there are strangely few places in New York with the picturesqueness of an earlier day. There are a few fine old churches and public buildings, of which City Hall is perhaps the most distinguished; there are some charming private houses of the pre-brownstone era here and there, especially in the Washington Square district. But New Yorkers have shown little taste for the decorous and agreeable, whether old or new; and as the city marched northward, it obliterated its own history as it went, tearing down the old dwelling to make way for the new office building, and then razing that in its turn to make way for the still newer skyscraper. (An immense amount of American social history has taken place in New York, but the spots where it occurred are mostly not only unmarked but unmarkable; the memorable buildings have mostly been swallowed up in new developments.) As the northward push continued, trees were remorselessly removed as unbecoming to a metropolis; only within the past two decades have New Yorkers waked up belatedly to the fact that trees add to the comeliness of urban life, and begun laboriously planting them again along parts of Fifth and Park Avenues and along some of the cross streets. Only within the past fifteen years, for that matter, has the city begun to demonstrate that it could produce anew an effect of gracious intimacy, as in the gardens leading down to the sunken plaza at Rockefeller Center—a place crowded all summer with people who feel obscurely that gaiety reigns here and spirits are restored—and even this spot appeals to them less, perhaps, for its jocundity than for its spectacular surroundings.

If you would look for what is really typical of New York,

28

Diorama, Museum of Natural History

do not look for expressions of the serene and disciplined life, of the backward-looking and contentment-seeking impulses: look for expressions of the restless and untrammeled imagination.

Look, for example, at the famous metropolitan skyline as it appears from the deck of a ferry; or, better still, go to the Hotel Bossert roof in Brooklyn and watch the scene across the East River when the dusk begins to draw in and the lights to sparkle in the tall buildings of Wall Street. A great deal has been written about that skyline—but not too much. For this cluster of soaring pinnacles is the very symbol of American aspiration. True, it has been, in part, a result of rising land-values, of commercial gregariousness, of organized greed if you will; but if the problem which it answered was economic, the answer was bold and brilliant and beautiful.

The view from almost any window high up in a midtown or uptown hotel will give you the same sense of looking at the embodiments of an imagination which has defied ordinary common sense. Especially at night, the spangled effects are among the wonders of the American world. New York specializes in producing extraordinary effects with light. To see what it can accomplish when it does this deliberately, don't miss the gaudy dazzle of Times Square of an evening, when the sidewalks are jammed with people out for a good time and the big electric signs with their unashamedly commercial messages make a glare almost as of daylight. But to see what delicate and unearthly beauty the city can convey without such premeditation, go rather into Central Park at dusk and look at the bank of skyscrapers along Central Park South. In the half-light they don't in the least look like the abode of human beings; you seem rather to be staring at a fantastic illuminated backdrop designed by a wildly imaginative artist trying to suggest the glitter of heaven.

The range of attractions for the visitor to New York is very wide. A great many people are satisfied to confine themselves to the shops, theaters, and night clubs; in the latter, certainly, the out-of-towners outnumber the native Manhattanites. For those

Statue of Liberty

who would look about a little more, the favorite sights tradition-
ally have been the Statute of Liberty, the Planetarium, the Little
Church Around the Corner, and of course Rockefeller Center
(including the Radio City Music Hall—if you can get in—and
the rhythmical Rockettes). But the museums are splendid, too; the
Zoo in the Bronx is worth seeing if you can spare the energy for
the trip from Manhattan; or if you can't, there is a delightful pint-
size zoolet in Central Park just off Fifth Avenue in the Sixties.
And of course in a city as multifarious as this, the visitor with
almost any special interest is likely to find something well worth
his or her individual attention, whether this be the Washington
Market at night, or the Stock Exchange, or the superb medical
centers, or La Guardia Airport, or Columbia University, or the
almost Parisian sidewalk cafés along lower Fifth Avenue in the
summertime, or the tours through the NBC studios in the RCA
Building, or the art dealers' galleries on Fifty-seventh Street, or
Coney Island, or—if you have a car and don't mind a long drive
along the fine parkways—Jones Beach, which is possibly the most
ingeniously designed big public recreation place in the world.

But as my mind runs over these wide-ranging possibilities,
it keeps coming back to the things that seem to me most intensely
characteristic of the city; and especially to something that is given
only passing mention, if any, in the guidebooks and is ignored
by thousands quite without notice.

Go to Park Avenue between Forty-sixth Street and Fiftieth
street, and as you turn off into any of the side streets, look down
through the gratings in the sidewalk. You will see railroad tracks.
Then reflect that within the memory of middle-aged people
this whole region—this imperial thoroughfare and the immense
hotels and office buildings which line it—was a train yard. (I have
before me a copy of Baedeker's *United States* published in 1899;
it says, "For the next ten blocks or so Park Avenue, or what would
otherwise be Park Avenue, is occupied by the various lines of
railway issuing from the Grand Central Depot.") The railroad
was electrified; the big power station was torn down and replaced

32

by a new one far underground in the solid rock; and without interrupting the train service the engineers built foundations between the tracks which would carry the steel frameworks on which huge buildings—to say nothing of streets—could be hung. These buildings have no cellars; even the front part of the enormous Waldorf is built right over the railroad tracks. Look down through those gratings and you can see for yourself.

There you have, it seems to me, a perfect exhibit of what is perhaps the most distinctive of our American assets: the ability to apply dauntless imagination to the solution of an engineering problem—the sort of ability that produced the Ford assembly line, the TVA, and the planning for D-Day. New York abounds in examples of it: the crowding towers of Wall Street; the city-within-a-city that is Rockefeller Center; the bridges, from Roebling's pioneer Brooklyn Bridge to the George Washington and the even more graceful Bronx-Whitestone Bridge east of La Guardia Field; and the great motor parkways created by the driving will power of Robert Moses. But this particular example somehow especially appeals to the imagination because it so nearly conceals itself. And even more than the others it reminds us that this city which in so many respects is our national headquarters inevitably lives and prospers less by its natural advantages of location than by the imaginative quality of the leadership which it can offer—leadership which, because so often expressed in decisions on paper, is not always visible to the casual eye. Let that leadership become timid, perfunctory, visionless, and the thousand pinnacles of New York will soon be aging monuments to the days when it expressed the unterrified forward thrust of the American genius; let it continue to grapple with necessity as boldly as these engineers grappled with the necessity of taking traffic across the rivers that surround Manhattan, or building a roaring avenue and mighty buildings on top of a railroad, and this city will continue to be the citadel of promise.

New York City

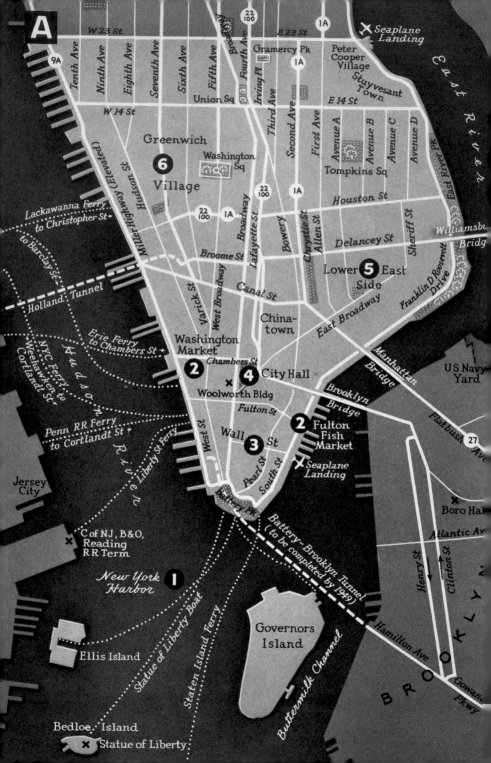

SECTION **A**

Lower Manhattan

(to 23rd Street)

LOWER MANHATTAN is at once the oldest and the newest part of the nation's largest city. The section's northern boundary—23rd Street—was outside the town's northern limits as late as Revolutionary War days. The tide of growth has carried the city's outposts from this modest civic birthplace to an area totaling 320 square miles. Still there are to be found here not only mementoes of the metropolis' very earliest days, but evidence as well, in Wall Street, City Hall and housing developments, of the newest metropolitan trends of today and tomorrow.

The outline map above relates Section A to Manhattan as a whole. The stories on the following pages are numbered to correspond with black-circled numbers that locate them on the Section A map (opposite). On pages 108-119 are pictures and text describing additional points of interest in this area.

This section is approached by all of New York's transportation facilities, most unusual being the ferries from Staten Island and New Jersey railroad terminals. Broadway, the city's best-known thoroughfare, starts at the Battery and bisects all Manhattan, becoming U.S. Highway No. 9 above the George Washington Bridge.

The Harbor

WITHIN A 25-MILE RADIUS of the Statue of Liberty (opposite page), lies the reason for New York City's being. Into the great harbor came early Dutch explorers, bent on trade and commerce. Because of the harbor s natural advantages of size and situation, industry prospered over the decades and pushed outward in all directions, up Manhattan Island from the first docks on South Street, out into New Jersey and Staten Island, out on Long Island toward the ocean. Expanding business pushed upward, too, erecting skyscrapers and great factories against the sky, and downward into the waters and the land, hewing out tunnels as other connecting links between units of what now is the nation's preeminent commercial community.

In this port area 11 million people live and upwards of 40,000 industrial establishments produce some seven billions of dollars worth of manufactured products each year. In and out of the port are moved the staggering total of 130,000,000 tons of goods a year. Ships bearing automobiles from Detroit and flour from Minnesota, headed for the open ocean 17 miles away, slip by battered freighters bearing coffee from Brazil and champagne from France. (The port moves more tonnage than the Houston, Baltimore, San Francisco Bay and Philadelphia areas combined; six of the world's greatest harbors could be placed within its boundaries with ease.) The 400,000 people who daily cross over, under and on the Hudson—in itself another connecting link with inland America, the Great Lakes and the St. Lawrence—see the huge piers which line both sides of the river, watch smutty-nosed tugs warping great ships into their berths and maneuvering them from pier to pier, look at railroad cars floating by to Manhattan docks, and perhaps catch a thrilling glimpse of some queen ship like the *Queen Elizabeth* serenely moving out to open water.

The harbor is the busy core, and at the same time the master, of the city. It forced railroads to go partially water borne so that goods could be brought to Manhattan from the Jersey terminals. It necessitated great spans like the George Washington Bridge so that visitors and commuters could reach Manhattan with ease. It sent huskies down into the river muck to build tunnels, like the Lincoln and the Holland, so that a flood of people and vehicles could come to the city of skyscrapers. It launched the ferryboat.

For an expenditure of five cents and 20 minutes, the Staten Island Ferry, from South Ferry, Manhattan, provides the best view of this colossus. On the right as the ferry pulls out into the Upper Bay, marked by the Whitehall Building, is the cavernous mouth of the Hudson River (called the North River to 14th St.), along both sides of which stretch the large piers; on the west side of the river are stacked industrial Weehawken, Hoboken and, lower, Jersey City. In the bay, on the right, are Ellis Island's dull brick buildings, where immigrants used to land, then Bedloe Island and the Statue of Liberty. To the left is Governors Island with neat brick Colonial structures for the U.S. Army; it sprawls at the mouth of the East River, where the first sailing vessels docked. Up the East River, the Brooklyn, Manhattan and Williamsburg Bridges, connecting Manhattan with Brooklyn, seem to merge above the docks.

Now, in the middle of the harbor with scurrying tankers and tugs, car floats and barges, you are in the very center of activity of the world's busiest port. To the right are the industrial plants and docks of Bayonne, behind which lie Newark and Elizabeth on Newark Bay, which is connected with the Upper Bay by Kill Van Kull, separating Bayonne from Staten Island. To the left lies Brooklyn with its colorful waterfront names: Red Hook, Gowanus Bay, Bay Ridge. As you continue straight ahead to St. George on Staten Island, outbound ships veer left through the Narrows, the wasp-waist link between Upper and Lower Bay, between Staten Island and Brooklyn. The Narrows will deliver them to the Lower Bay, under the western end of Long Island, and the Ambrose Channel, thence to the ocean. The five-mile return trip from Staten Island will bring you back to one of the city's most rewarding views, lower Manhattan's spires rising from the waters.

The Statue of Liberty can be visited by boats leaving from the Battery. Another view of the city's waterways is available by three-hour trips around Manhattan from Battery Landing and West 42nd St. docks. These take one past the Battery; up the East River (a 16-mile estuary connecting the Upper Bay with Long Island Sound) under the Brooklyn, Manhattan and Williamsburg Bridges, with the U.S. Navy Yard on the right; past long, slender Welfare Island with its hospitals and Queensboro Bridge; Wards and Randalls Islands which support the magnificent engineering of the Triborough Bridge; up the Harlem River along Manhattan's top, past coal hoists, the Polo Grounds and wooded parks to the salty Hudson, the port's only true river. Down the Hudson is the 600-foot-high George Washington Bridge and, on the right, the spectacular Palisades and then industrial Jersey, with Weehawken ferry and freight sheds. On the left, on Manhattan, are the ribbon parks and the port's largest piers, for ocean liners, the larger freighters and, at the island's tip near the Battery, the fruit boats and then the Upper Bay again.

The Statue of Liberty on Bedloe Island dominates the harbor as it looks toward Brooklyn and the sea. The 225-ton, 151-foot high

statue was presented by the French people and dedicated in 1886. The upheld arm with burning torch is 330 feet above the sea.

Governors Island looks across 500 yards of water to Manhattan. Dominated by Fort Jay, it is Army headquarters for the area.

Ellis Island, near the Jersey shore, received more than a million immigrants in its peak year. Now it is used as a detention center.

The tugboats are the work-horses of the harbor. Nothing is too big (the *Queen Elizabeth*) or too little (a scow). Here a boat is being nudged into the Hudson. Tug men are hardy, and wise in the ways of the complicated harbor; many have worked in the port for 40 years and more. A good sized Diesel-powered tug carries seven men, often costs more than $150,000.

45

Hudson docks receive the ocean liners like the *Queen Mary*, which

can now be outfitted for return trips in as little as 36 hours.

The harbor created this metropolis: Manhattan in center; the Hud-

son River and New Jersey, left; Long Island (right) across the river.

The Waterfront

UP FROM THE HARBOR and the Battery runs West Street (opposite page), main gateway into the city for water-borne traffic. At the foot of the street, overlooking Governors Island (upper left) and the Upper Bay's scurrying ships, is the Whitehall Building, where many maritime enterprises have their offices, from which the Moran Company keeps an eye on its tugs that nudge big boats to their piers, and from the roof of which the Government checks the all-important weather. Across the street, at the far tip, lies ancient Pier A, where are berthed the police and fire-boats that protect the shipping which has made West Street's waterfront the site of the greatest collection of marine endeavors on the globe.

Just above Pier A are the docks of fruit boats from the south, bringing oranges and bananas to New York and all America. Above them are the berths of railroad scows, carrying across the river produce to be sold on the piers. (Every year more than 100,-000,000 tons of freight are moved in or out of the port by 12 railroads, only two of which have approaches to the city by land.) Farther up, trans-Atlantic liners dock. The complete port has a waterfront of 651 miles.

Although a great deal of the cargo, valued at about ten billion dollars a year, is trans-shipped to the remainder of the nation, staggering amounts are required to feed and outfit New Yorkers, who drink three and a half million quarts of milk a day and consume three million loaves of bread. Long Island produce is trucked in, too. These trucks, and others, fill the market streets early each morning. One of the most colorful of the city's 20 wholesale areas is the Washington Market, north of Fulton St., which sprawls between and around West and Greenwich Streets. (See next page.) The city-owned Washington Retail Market is notable for the wide variety of domestic and imported foods available in leased stalls. Farther uptown, the Gansevoort Market, at Little West Twelfth St., opens for business at 4 A.M. with farmers from nearby rural areas offering tomatoes, beans, lettuce and other produce. Butter and eggs are sold in the Mercantile Exchange at Hudson and Harrison Streets; poultry commission houses are near Reade St. and, farther north, odors of tea, spices and coffee fill the air. Wholesale leather firms are clustered on Reade and Duane Streets; across town, around the intersection of South and Fulton Streets, is the city's most noted single enterprise, the Fulton Fish Market.

Besides the North River and East River waterfronts, there are the Newtown Creek area which separates Brooklyn and Long Island City; Brooklyn's important development from Newtown Creek to Bay Ridge with immense facilities for industrial plants, dry-docking, ship repairing and freight handling, highlighted by the New York Dock Co. and the Bush Terminal—complete with warehouses and loft buildings; the Jersey side of Staten Island; and, of course, tremendous New Jersey developments.

The deluge of freight directed at these various fronts, and the resulting variety of costly and inefficient ways evolved to handle it, brought about the creation in 1921 of the Port of New York Authority to simplify and unify operations on a bi-state regional basis. This agency has been highly successful, but the surface appearance of turmoil and tumult on the waterfront is still one of New York's best free shows.

Into the docks on the North (lower Hudson) River come freighters with produce for the city's waterfront markets. More than 10,000 such vessels steam up the harbor to piers like these each year.

This sea-struck boy gets a closer look. Floats with freight cars from
the west side of the Hudson also dock on the North River.

54

The West Side elevated highway slopes down into West Street. At
left is the North River; to the right. the Washington Market.

Onions from Idaho and hundreds of other items pour into the Lower West Side to make the Washington Produce Market the largest in

the world. Before most of the city awakens, perishable goods are displayed, sold and moved out amid bustle and noise.

Across town, South Street (seen here from the Brooklyn Bridge) swerves close to Wall Street's skyscrapers as it parallels the East River. The modernism of the skyscraper at 120 Wall Street (left) contrasts with old buildings at its feet.

The six-block Fulton market, established in 1821, has an air—and a flavor — especially in the sheds where fish are cleaned.

Its people, too, are salty characters, like this old fisherman working where early settlers of New York docked their boats.

One hundred varieties are brought to the Fulton Fish Market on
South Street and the East River by trawlers and refrigerated trucks

from New England and Jersey. In the shadow of Brooklyn Bridge men daily clean, bone, ice and pack fish before 9 A.M.

Wall Street

WALL STREET, once the city's fortified northern boundary, now is the place where big skyscrapers grow. A third of a mile long, the narrow canyon runs through the financial district's towering shapes from the East River to Trinity Church. These high buildings, rising above the waterways that first brought the city to commercial importance, indicate the metropolis' contemporary pre-eminence in trade, shipping and finance.

The towers are rooted in historic soil. Here the first president of the United States was inaugurated, on April 30, 1789, where the Subtreasury Building now stands at Wall and Nassau Streets. On the same site, in 1735, John Peter Zenger was acquitted of libeling the governor and became the nation's first hero of press freedom.

The Wall Street district provides the nation with centralized credit and banking facilities and a sales place for securities; it is also one of the great money capitals of the world. Financing for an industry of the future may be arranged close to the spot where Alexander Hamilton in 1784 organized the city's first bank, the Bank of New York and Trust Co., now at 48 Wall. The world's greatest Stock Exchange grew from an outdoor market under a buttonwood tree at what is now 68 Wall in 1792 to the four famous buildings covering the area between New, Wall and Broad Streets and Exchange Place. On the trading floor of the Exchange securities are bought and sold in a matter of moments. Orders are sent to brokerage houses which relay them to their members on the floor; these men conduct business orally with other members. Transactions are quickly noted on the Exchange's ticker tape. Securities listed on the Exchange are valued at more than 200 billions, and annual transactions soar into the hundreds of millions of shares. There are some 1400 brokers, whose seats on the Exchange have varied in price from $625,000 to $17,000. These figures suggest something of the dramatic ups and downs in its history: Black Friday (Sept. 24, 1869), a result of Jay Gould's and Jim Fiske's attempt to corner the gold market; the collapses of 1901 and 1907; the panic of October, 1929. Trading can be watched from a gallery.

Other markets in the financial district include the Curb Exchange, 78 Trinity Place; the Cotton Exchange, 60 Beaver Street, world's most important cotton market; the Maritime Exchange and Commodity Exchange at 80 and 81 Broad Street; the Coffee and Sugar Exchange at 113 Pearl Street.

On following pages are shown some of the financial district's most important buildings. More than 50,000 work here in skyscrapers. Just before 9 A.M., narrow streets are filled with office personnel—clerks and tellers, stenographers and office boys —who have come from their homes by means of ferry, elevated railway, subway or bus. Soon the brokers, the bankers, insurance men, the lawyers, the engineers and the many other types of specialists required by this specialized business arrive by car, by plane—or by subway. Many wear the standard uniform, conservative suit and coat, Homburg hat, black umbrella. The most successful break their work day with lunch at the Down Town Association, or at Fraunces Tavern, another link with Wall Street's storied past, which also houses a museum and library devoted to Revolutionary history, including George Washington's solemn farewell to his brothers in arms, which took place here. Thus the district, as demonstrated also in the pictures that follow, is a study in contrasts of old and new.

Some commuting businessmen land planes here in the shadow of skyscrapers where Wall Street runs into the East River.

The financial district's canyons twist east from Broadway. This is Exchange Place, with the Central Hanover Bank and Trust Company Building at left. Down the block, at 45 Broadway, is the reputed site of the first white man's residence on Manhattan.

J. Q. A. Ward's Statue of George Washington, in front of the Sub-treasury Building, looks across Wall Street to the Stock Exchange.

965-foot-high 60 Wall Tower is at left; Bank of New York (right).

Curb Exchange and Trinity Churchyard (left); at right, 99 John St.

Woolworth Bldg., once the world's tallest, overlooks City Hall.

Wall Street begins at Trinity Church and its famous burying ground, with First National Bank at left and Irving Trust at right.

Bas-relief decorations on Trinity's bronze doors depict symbolic scenes from the Bible (above) and events in church history. Queen Anne, in 1705, gave the parish a grant of land which eventually made it one of the world's wealthiest. The present Episcopal worshiping place was built in 1846. Only 79 feet wide and 166 feet long, the spired brownstone structure is a downtown landmark.

An early rector of Trinity, the Rev. Morgan Dix, is memorialized in Dix Chapel (left). Alexander Hamilton's grave is marked (right).

George Washington bade farewell to his officers in 1783 here in the Long Room of the Fraunces Tavern, at Pearl and Broad Streets.

Nearby, at the foot of Broadway in Bowling Green, is the bronze statue of Abraham de Peyster, merchant and early mayor of the city.

Up Broadway is St. Paul's Chapel, oldest church in the city.

St. Paul's appears spacious because of its barrel vault.

Washington's pew is marked by a painting of U.S. Coat of Arms.

City Hall District

CITY HALL PARK, an historic site one mile north of the Battery, is New York's village green. Here Colonial citizens gathered to agitate against the Stamp Act and erect a Liberty Pole; here the Declaration of Independence was read in the presence of George Washington.

Although the city has gradually sprawled northward, this section remains the center of New York's governmental activities. On the north side of the park is City Hall (opposite page), New York's third civic building, completed in 1811. An excellent example of post-Colonial architecture, City Hall houses offices of the Mayor, the City Council and Board of Estimate. On the steps outside, distinguished visitors are welcomed and other official ceremonies are held.

City Court Building, directly behind City Hall, was built by the infamous Tweed Ring (1861-72). Its cost, more than $12,000,000, provided one of the city's biggest graft scandals. The Hall of Records, at Chambers and Centre Streets, contains documents of land transactions dating back to 1653.

East of City Hall Park is all that remains of Newspaper Row, late nineteenth century publishing center. The *World,* now defunct, flourished in the gilt-domed Pulitzer Building near the entrance to Brooklyn Bridge; the *Tribune* was once published at Spruce and Nassau Streets. Only the *Sun,* in the Stewart Building northwest of the park, remains in the area.

In a circle facing Foley Square, northeast of City Hall Park, lie the imposing buildings which make up the Civic Center, headquarters for State, Federal and municipal business.

Inside City Hall, a flying staircase leads to the upper gallery and the Governors' Suite, a museum devoted to historical relics.

Left: County and Federal (with tower) courthouses face Foley Sq.
Right: Criminal Courts Building (background) and State Office.

The 40-story Municipal Building (center) looks on City Hall and
the park which forms a triangle between Broadway and Park Row.

79

The Lower East Side

THE LOWER EAST SIDE is rich and colorful—with foreign restaurants, sidewalk bazaars and street festivals—but it is also a district of tenement slums, cold-water flats and congested streets. Complex and diverse in its social and physical structure, the Lower East Side presents, in a compressed area, most of the aspects of metropolitan life.

In the days of New Amsterdam, there were swampy meadows along the East River, and a large part of the Lower East Side was occupied by Peter Stuyvesant's farm. It was not until the last half of the nineteenth century that the section fully entered its so-called "melting pot" phase when large numbers of Germans and Irish moved in, followed by Russians, Italians, Slavs and Jews. Leveling-off of immigration came in the 1920's.

The Lower East Side has many distinct neighborhoods. The Bowery (pp. 86-89), once an Indian trail and the only land entrance to New York during the Revolution, is a dingy stripe through the section which divides Chinatown and Little Italy on the west from the Jewish quarter on the east. Today's Bowery is a haven for the destitute, for panhandlers and sidewalk hawkers. At No. 227 is Bowery Mission, some 60 years old, and at No. 267 is Sammy's Bowery Follies, a flourishing night club.

Chinatown (pp. 90-91), inhabited by 6,000 Chinese, forms the nucleus of the 48,000 Chinese in Greater New York. Importers on Pell, Mott and Doyer Streets sell oriental wares, and shop windows are piled high with Chinese herbs, shark fins, and roast ducks. Chinatown publishes five newspapers and has its own school at 64 Mott Street, where children are taught the language and traditions of their ancestors after regular school hours. There is a Chinese movie house and an opera house which stages Chinese dramas.

Mulberry Street is the center of Little Italy (pp. 92-95), a section of ill-ventilated dwellings with grimy clotheslines and littered fire escapes. Shops in the neighborhood sell Italian delicacies such as goat's cheeses and pizza.

Knickerbocker Village (p. 118), an immense housing project with 1,600 apartments, lies southeast of the Bowery at Cherry and Catharine Streets in the old Fourth Ward District. Nearby, at 265 Henry, is the main building of the famous Henry Street Settlement, founded in 1893 by Lillian Wald.

The Jewish quarter (p. 85) covers a wide area between the Bowery and the East River with its tiny shops, synagogues, chain stores and crowded tenements. Here, sidewalk stalls sell hot *knishes,* yard goods, hardware and notions. Brass Town (p.119) on Allen Street below Delancey, displays copper, brass and other metal objects. The structure of the Williamsburg Bridge rises at Clinton and Delancey Streets. Farther uptown, on Second Avenue from Houston to 14th Street, is the Jewish Rialto, with many foreign restaurants, movie houses and theaters. The Café Royal, 188 Second Avenue, is a meeting-place for Jewish actors and intellectuals.

The slum area of the old "gashouse district," above 14th Street on the East River, has given way to the large housing projects of Stuyvesant Town and Peter Cooper Village. Fourteenth Street, known for theaters and fine restaurants in the late 1800's, is crowded with retail stores, movie houses and soft-drink stands. Union Square (page 96) is a downtown shopping center for low-priced women's clothes. Its leading establishments are Ohrbach's and Klein's.

Gramercy Park (p. 113), a fenced-in private park at Irving Place and 20th Street, is the fashionable residential section of the Lower East Side. Spacious red-brick and brownstone houses overlook the small park on all four sides.

Noisy streets and crowded tenements like these are characteristic of the Lower East Side, which extends roughly from City Hall District north to 23rd St. and from Broadway to the East River. Some slums are gradually giving way to modern housing projects.

The Lower East Side has many foreign neighborhoods within its bounds. Madison Street (above) is the center of a Greek community.

Housewives in the Jewish section shop at outdoor markets. Stalls of Orchard Street Market line several blocks above and below Delancey Street, main artery of the district. Pushcarts like the one above, at Hester and Suffolk Streets, are rapidly disappearing.

Signs on and near the Bowery advertise outsize and bargain suits . . .

. . . as well as barber "college" haircuts and kosher provisions.

Along the Bowery, from Chatham Square to East 4th St., rescue missions offer food and lodging to down-and-outers, saloons sell a popular drink called "smoke," and restaurants serve 20-cent meals.

The Third Avenue El, Manhattan's last elevated, casts dark shadows on Third Avenue and the Bowery. El trains rumble past second-

story windows of dancehalls and flophouses, stop for passengers at gabled station houses heated in winter by pot-bellied stoves.

South of Bayard St., just off the Bowery, are the five triangular
blocks of Chinatown. Tourists dine in Chinese restaurants and . . .

. . . visit a temple on Mott St., where souvenirs are sold before an enormous Buddha (above) and other religious images.

Little Italy, just north of Chinatown, holds many church festivals.
During a celebration, San Ganarro (above) receives gifts of money.

On feast days, streets of the district are decorated with colored
electric lights; bands play for parades in honor of patton saints.

As many as 50,000 people turn out for church-day festivities in Little Italy. Dancing in the streets (above) is part of the fun.

Merrymakers take time out to buy souvenirs and food at sidewalk booths. The proprietor of the stand above hawks Italian sausage.

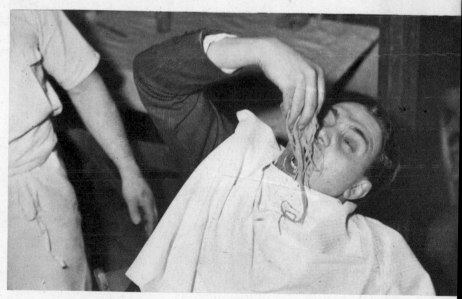

Most popular feast-day foods are spaghetti, spaghettini, linguina and ziti lobsters, accompanied by olives, finochio and sweets.

Union Square Park, which begins at 14th St. and extends from Fourth Ave. west to Broadway, is frequented by working people and downtown shoppers. In the foreground above is a statue of George Washington; behind it rises the Liberty Pole, erected in 1924.

St. Mark's In-the-Bouwerie, at Second Ave. and East 10th St., began as a chapel on Peter Stuyvesant's farm, was rebuilt in 1799.

97

Greenwich Village

GREENWICH VILLAGE, once characterized by artistic revolt and intellectual radicalism, has ceased fermenting of recent years and is settling down into a rather staid urban community. Although the Village still has its "bohemians," writers and artists, the majority of its residents are family people, white-collar workers and professionals. The early charm of the Village remains, however, in its rambling streets, quaint shops and old houses with gabled roofs and chimney pots.

The Village covers a wide area west of Broadway below 14th St., with focal points at Washington and Sheridan Squares. Colonial New Yorkers, among them Brevoorts, Bleeckers and Bayards, built estates in the section, and in the 1700's yellow fever epidemics drove scores of citizens uptown from the Battery to the healthier Village. From earliest days, Greenwich Village has had its literary life—Poe, Paine and Whitman all lived here —but its artistic and intellectual heyday began about 1910 and continued through the early '30's. The biannual outdoor art show in Washington Square (see opposite page) is one of the institutions established during this period.

At the foot of Fifth Avenue, the 86-foot-high Washington Arch (see color photograph in Introduction), built in honor of Washington's first inaugural, marks the Washington Square section of Greenwich Village. The Square itself was a potter's field in the late 1700's and became a landscaped park about 1827. Today, its park benches, shaded by oaks and elms, are meeting places for students from New York University on the east and Villagers from the west and south. Dignified red-brick homes on

Washington Square North, dating from the early 1800's, have been occupied by well-known families and by writers such as Henry James and Edith Wharton. MacDougal Alley, half a block north of Washington Square on the west, is lined with studios and homes converted from ancient mews. On Washington Square South is the yellow-brick Judson Memorial Church, with a lighted cross on its tower.

The Washington Square section has several old hotels noted for excellent food and distinguished clientele. Best known are the Hotel Brevoort (p. 107), at Fifth Avenue and 8th St., and the Hotel Lafayette, at University Place and 9th St.

Eighth St., the "Main Street" of Greenwich Village, is crowded with shops from Fifth Ave. to Sixth. Here tourists may browse in antique shops, bookstores, art galleries, and jewelry stores which sell articles fashioned in the neighborhood. The pink-façaded Whitney Museum of American Art, 10 West 8th St., is noted for its encouragement and display of the work of living American artists.

One of the city's Italian sections begins south of Washington Square and extends as far as Spring Street. Villagers frequent the many restaurants of this community and shop at colorful fruit and vegetable stands.

The district which centers in Sheridan Square, at the juncture of Seventh Ave. and West 4th St., is celebrated for its night life. After dark, the Square and adjacent streets blaze with lights beckoning tourists into restaurants, bars and night clubs, which offer hot music and variety floor shows. "Real Villagers," including eccentrics of the neighborhood, meet in cafeterias and lunch wagons in the vicinity.

On the winding streets south of Sheridan Square are many old New York houses with steep slate roofs, brass doorknobs and gardens in the rear. Set down among them, at 27 Barrow St., is Greenwich House, noted for settlement work and an experimental nursery school.

Mark Twain once lived in this house at Fifth Ave. and 9th St. To the north, at 10th St., is the Church of the Ascension.

The Village has many studios like those on 10th St. (above left).
City's narrowest house (right), 75½ Bedford St., is 9′ 6″ across.

Old homes on Grove St. date back to the early 1800's. A gate leads
to the wood and brick houses of Grove Court, built about 1830.

St. Luke's Chapel, built 1821-22, faces Grove St. on Hudson St.
Inside, near the font, is an ancient statue of Saint Christopher.

103

Homes that once were stables line Washington Mews on lower Fifth.

Women delinquents are tried at Jefferson Market Court, a Victorian Gothic building at the juncture of West 10th St., Sixth and Greenwich Avenues. Adjoining is the House of Detention for Women.

Ailanthus trees shade the old brick houses that line Patchin Place, a blind alley accessible from West 10th St. near Sixth Ave.

Villagers meet to discuss art and literature at restaurants like the one shown above, on MacDougal St. west of Washington Square.

Several lower Fifth Ave. hotels have sidewalk cafes for warm-weather dining, among them the Hotel Brevoort at Eighth St.

Other Points of Interest

CHERRY LANE THEATER—Revivals of Broadway successes are staged at the Cherry Lane Theater, 38 Commerce St., just off Seventh Ave. below Sheridan Square. Converted from an old barn, the theater was an experimental workshop for the New Playwrights group in the period following World War I.

CHURCH OF ST. ANDREW—A new church, built in 1938, replaces the 120-year-old original Roman Catholic St. Andrew's at Duane St. and Cardinal Pl. on old Newspaper Row. Printers on the night shifts of the great dailies formerly published in the neighborhood used to attend 2:30 A.M. Masses here.

CHURCH OF ST. NICHOLAS—Between Washington and West Streets on Cedar is a little Greek Orthodox church which dates back to 1820. A colorful ceremony is performed each year on the Day of Epiphany (January 6) when a wooden cross is thrown into the harbor from the Battery and symbolically rescued.

CITY FIREBOAT STATION—At the west end of the sea wall below the Battery is the harbor's firehouse; berthed beside it are the 10 fireboats which protect the city's waterfront. A lookout tower tops the two-story building.

COMMUNICATIONS BUILDING—At Sixth Ave. near Walker St. on the Lower West Side is the Long Distance Building of the American Telephone and Telegraph Co. All private telephone and teletype wires out of New York City go through this building to the nation and to foreign cities. The largest communications center in the world, it is the junction of many telephone trunk lines and center of many radio networks.

CUNARD BUILDING—Ship models of every type of Cunard vessel from the first paddle wheeler to the *Queen Mary* are on display in the main office of this 22-story building at 25 Broadway. Historic murals decorate the ceiling, and old maps line the walls.

CUSTOM HOUSE—Marble statues, representing four continents, line the front of the seven-story U.S. Customs building across from Bowling Green, at the foot of Broadway. Located here are offices of the Collector of Customs for the Port of New York, of the Comptroller of Customs, Collector of Internal Revenue, Coast Guard and Tariff Commission. Famous buildings formerly on this site were Fort Amsterdam and a structure intended for George Washington. Paintings and murals in the interior of the present structure include Elmer E. Garnsey's noted "Seventeenth Century Ports."

EQUITABLE BUILDING—The 40-story structure, with more than a billion feet of office space, has the city's highest assessment: 29 million.

FEDERAL HALL MEMORIAL MUSEUM—On the ground floor of the many-columned Subtreasury Building on Wall St. is a historical museum containing relics of George Washington and paintings of old New York. Washington's watch, his family china and the stone on which he stood when delivering the first inaugural address are here preserved.

FLATIRON BUILDING—Wedged into the shape of a flatiron by the intersection of Broadway and Fifth Ave. at 23rd St., the 21-story Fuller Building at Madison Square was considered a skyscraper when it was built in 1902.

GRACE CHURCH—This early Episcopal church, dedicated in 1846, is at the corner of Tenth St. and Broadway. The exterior of the English Gothic building is richly ornamented with carvings.

INDIA HOUSE—This old structure at 1 Hanover Square in the Wall St. District was built in 1837 as a private club for foreign merchants. It now contains many ship models and old prints. and a restaurant frequented by Wall Streeters.

MONEYS OF THE WORLD—The Chase National Bank at 46 Cedar St. has on display a collection of coins and currencies ranging from wooden nickels and worthless continentals to the latest dime and thousand dollar bill. It is open to the public, 9:00 A.M. to 4:00 P.M.

MORGAN BUILDING—J. P. Morgan & Co., Inc., the best known banking house in America, is located in a small, austere five-story building across from the Stock Exchange, at 23 Wall St.

NEW SCHOOL FOR SOCIAL RESEARCH—This many-windowed modernistic building, at 66 West Twelfth St., houses a school specializing in adult studies. Emphasis is on political science, the social sciences and psychology. Many refugee scholars exiled from Nazi Germany taught here during the war. The new building, erected in 1931, is an unusual example of modern architecture and contains interesting examples of modern paintings by Thomas Benton, the Mexican Orozco and Camilo Egas, of Ecuador.

NEW YORK TELEPHONE COMPANY BUILDING—Thirty-two stories high and 52,000 square feet in area, this handsome building at 140 West St. is the largest telephone building in the world.

NEW YORK UNIVERSITY — The downtown branch of N.Y.U. is located on the east side of Washington Square on the original site of the university, which was founded in 1830. The three main buildings contain a liberal arts college, the school of commerce and the school of education, with day, evening and summer classes. N.Y.U.'s other campus is at University Heights in the Bronx. (See pp. 310-319.)

POLICE HEADQUARTERS — This large French Baroque building at the head of Centre St. between Grand and Broome on the Lower East Side is the main office of the 83 police precincts of the five city boroughs. Here are the offices of the Police Commissioner, the Missing Persons Bureau, three short-wave radio stations. The Police Academy across Broome St. trains New York's rookies.

ROOSEVELT HOUSE—The birthplace of Theodore Roosevelt, at 28 E. 20th St., has been made into a museum featuring family heirlooms and a library.

SINGER BUILDING—In 1908, when it was built, this 41-story office building at Broadway and John St. was the tallest in the city. Now it is sixteenth.

ST. PETER'S CHURCH—The oldest Roman Catholic Church building in Manhattan (1786, rebuilt 1838) is an imposing six-columned structure at the corner of Barclay and Church streets, now hemmed in by modern office buildings.

SPANISH-PORTUGUESE CEMETERIES—One block south of Chatham Square on New Bowery is the oldest Jewish cemetery in Manhattan. The plot was purchased in 1682 by Spanish and Portuguese Jews who had escaped to the New World from the Inquisition. The second Spanish-Portuguese Jewish Cemetery is located in Greenwich Village, just east of Sixth Ave. on 11th St.

STUYVESANT SQUARE—Originally a part of old Peter Stuyvesant's farm, this dignified little park between 15th and 17th streets is really two squares, divided by Second Ave. In the 1860's it was a center of wealthy homes; by the 90's it had been overrun by successive waves of German, Irish and Italian immigrants. Today it is surrounded by hospitals (Salvation Army, Beth Israel, Manhattan General, St. Andrew's, New York Infirmary) and church establishments (the Friends' Meeting House and Seminary; St. George's Protestant Episcopal Church; St. Dunstan's House, headquarters of a monastic Catholic sect; and the Convent of the Little Sisters of the Assumption).

WANAMAKER'S—One of the largest downtown department stores is John Wanamaker's at Broadway and 9th St. Its two old-fashioned buildings are joined by a three-level covered bridge over 9th St.

This statue of De Verrazano, who is believed to have entered New
York Harbor in 1524, stands in Battery Park, at Manhattan's tip.

In the Gramercy Park District, between 18th and 23rd Streets, brick houses with wrought iron porches were once owned by New York's most fashionable people, including Mrs. Stuyvesant Fish, social arbiter. Gramercy Park is still locked to the general public.

New York's oldest restaurant is Ye Olde Chop House on Cedar St.
Gen. Grant drank whisky at The Old Beekman, on Gold St.

McSorley's Old Ale House, east of Third Ave. at 15 E. 7th St., is
an especially noted tavern. It was established in 1854.

Noted for its Duncan Phyfe furniture is Old Merchant's House in
the Astor Place district at 29 E. 4th St., now open to the public.

Peter Cooper founded Cooper Union, at 4th Ave. and 7th St., in 1859 as a free school and forum. Lincoln spoke here in 1860.

Cooper Union's Museum for the Arts of Decoration includes the
18th century band (top) from Crete and portrait of Charles I.

117

Some of the worst Lower East Side slums have been replaced by such modern housing as Knickerbocker Village, built in the '30's.

On Allen Street, little shops like this feature brass and silver.

Open stalls with second-hand books line lower Fourth Avenue.

SECTION B

Midtown Manhattan
(from 23rd to 110th Streets)

MIDTOWN MANHATTAN contains the great business and pleasure industries of the city. It is bounded on the south by Greenwich Village and the Lower East Side, and on the north by the residential-university section and the three Harlems. The area includes many of the city's most important attractions—Times Square and its related entertainment areas, Rockefeller Center with its business and recreational facilities, the great rail terminals and large hotels.

The outline map above places Section B in relation to Manhattan. As in other parts of this book, the stories on the following pages bear numbers which correspond with numbers locating them on the map on the opposite page. Additional points of interest in the section are shown and described on pages 218-233.

Numbered avenues running north and south, and numbered streets running east and west, make this section easy to explore. Main cross streets are 34th (with the shopping center at Herald Square), 42nd with high points at Times Square and Fifth Avenue, 57th and 59th, which becomes Central Park South as it passes the southern tip of the park.

Times Square

TIMES SQUARE is the focal point of America's good time. It is the No. 1 tourist attraction in the nation's No. 1 tourist town. Here, at 42nd St. and Broadway, are the world's flashiest invitations to fun.

By daylight, Times Square is a clutter of skyscrapers, shabby buildings, soft-drink stands, souvenir shops and movie marquees with lights that feebly challenge the sun. But at dusk it changes into a swirl of animated signs seven stories high, flashing neon advertising, noisy hawkers, news spelled out on the Times Building, buses and taxis that pack Broadway, Seventh Ave., crosstown streets—and tens of thousands of people.

The heart of this turmoil—and of the entertainment business —is the legitimate theater. Its lustiest offspring, gargantuan movies, has forced it off once-opulent 42nd St. and even off Broadway into sidestreet playhouses. And even here its other child, radio, has taken over many of its theaters so that audiences may actually see radio programs. But still the theater remains. The movies' images, the radio's voice cannot often supply the stimulating relationship of audience and actor. In less than 40 playhouses, visitors and New Yorkers see Katharine Cornell and Helen Hayes, and next year's young star-to-be, in plays and musicals which, if they are accepted by critics and public, will later tour the country.

Just as the theater's influence spreads to movies, radio, television and popular music, so the theater's home base, Times Square, sprawls out into what is known as the Times Square District. This area, bounded by 42nd and 59th Streets and 5th and

8th Avenues, has over 50 million visitors a year who spend tens of millions of dollars in the show area.

The New York theater, since its beginning on Dec. 6, 1732, has been accustomed to packing up and moving. From its early location in lower Manhattan, it moved over the years upward from the Bowery along Broadway to its present site. Gaudy melodramas, classics, and minstrel shows were succeeded by the era of great names—actors Edwin Forrest, Edwin Booth, Ada Rehan, John Drew, Mrs. Gilbert, Sarah Bernhardt, Eleanora Duse, Ellen Terry, Maude Adams, the Barrymores, and by playwrights Ibsen and Shaw. Of importance was the pioneering work of such groups as the Provincetown Players, which first produced Eugene O'Neill; the Little Theater movement pioneered by the Neighborhood Playhouse; and the Washington Square Players which became the Theater Guild, today's largest producing organization.

But of New York's 688 theaters, seating over 800,000 patrons, the majority are now dedicated to the movies. However, today's mammoth Radio City Music Hall (pp. 145-147) is hardly related to the Kinetoscope Parlor which opened on April 14, 1894, for the showing of Edison's 50-foot films of Buffalo Bill and Annie Oakley, at a penny a view. Film was projected on a theater screen for the first public showing at Koster and Bial's Music Hall in New York in 1896. In and around New York the first movies were made, by Edison and the men who later built Hollywood. Among the results are million-dollar motion-picture palaces that line Broadway today.

Radio shows are available, too. Some are broadcast from Times Square theaters, others from studios in the networks' headquarters. Although Hollywood has become an important broadcasting center, New York has remained the home town of radio since 1909, when Dr. Lee De Forest set up a radiotelephone pickup of *Pagliacci,* with Caruso, at the Metropolitan Opera House and piped it to his home. Free tickets to broadcasts can be obtained (see Recreational Directory in the Appendix, p. 376).

Tours are conducted through Radio City, home of the National and American Broadcasting companies. Of interest is the television tour, which provides a glimpse of how America's newest entertainment device operates. Since 1927, when television pictures were sent from New York to Washington, the city has been a center for research; regular programs are now telecast.

The Times Square District's noisy speed is best expressed in another of the area's unique industries—Tin Pan Alley. The men who write a nation's songs necessarily have their headquarters here, close to the entertainment business. Here, too, are many of the night clubs and spots where their songs are played and sung in many tempos, but usually fast—and loud.

In most of the small clubs jammed on 52nd St., sole objectives are playing hot music—and listening to it. Here the greats of jazz have so played as to make almost legendary such club names as Onyx, Famous Door and Hickory House. Greenwich village, downtown, also has contributed to the story of hot music such names as Nick's and Eddie Condon.

In contrast are large theater restaurants near Broadway which offer loud music, a chance to dance and eat, pretty girls to look at and a show. Considerably more expensive and less noisy are the clubs of the East Side, most of them east of 5th Ave. Many of the large hotels have night clubs offering everything from swing through sweet to rumba music.

Tin Pan Alley's products receive their most strenuous renditions at big dance palaces such as the Savoy Ballroom in Harlem, where some of the most energetic jitterbugging the nation has ever seen is performed, and at Roseland on Broadway, where a dime will get you a dancing partner.

Times Square is truly a maelstrom which causes, and possibly cures, more headaches and heartaches than any similar entertainment area in the world.

New Year's Eve is the annual climax for Times Square. At this one moment, crowds are greatest, noises are loudest, in this favorite

gathering place for celebrations touched off by the *Times* news flashes on the building from which this picture was taken.

Broadway crowds like to eat, and they have their choice of Automat (above), orange-drink and hot-dog stands, or restaurants where they can get a snack or five courses. Whatever the place, the service is fast, because Times Square tempo is quick.

Shooting galleries and flea circuses enliven 42nd Street, once the heroine of a song and the proud avenue of theater hits.

Movie marquees on 42nd Street are designed to startle, to bedazzle and to entice. Horror pictures and comedies share mention.

Shubert Alley, named for the theatrical managers, connects 44th and 45th streets, heart of the theater district, west of Broadway.

In the Times Square District, shows that tour the nation make their bow. "Oklahoma!" (above) shares all-time long-run honors with "Tobacco Road," "Life with Father" and "Abie's Irish Rose." In the theater section, a tuneful girl show may be playing next to a revival of Ibsen or Shakespeare. The area is filled with hopeful young talent trying to break in to either type.

The variety of entertainment offered in the night spots on 52nd Street is indicated by the conglomeration of signs shown here.

East of Fifth Ave. on 53rd St., the Stork Club plays down its music
plays up its famous and near-famous guests in the Cub Room.

The 21 Club, on 52nd St., behind hitching posts and a grilled fence
of the Hockstader mansion, emphasizes excellent food, too.

133

Somewhat noisier are such huge dine-dance-and-show places as Billy Rose's Diamond Horseshoe, just off Broadway.

At El Morocco, on E. 54th St., tastes run to vintage wines. In such places, columnists on the Times Square beat gather items.

Rockefeller Center

ROCKEFELLER CENTER is the American Dream of Big City come true. Here thousands of men worked eight years, digging deep into 12 acres of city soil and rock, pushing toward the sky some 130 thousand tons of structural steel held together by 10 million rivets. The result, compounded of steel and concrete, limestone, aluminum and 56 other basic materials, is Rockefeller Center, the embodiment of what every tourist thinks New York should be.

From Fifth Ave., midway between 49th and 50th Streets, a "channel" with flower beds and fountains leads down between La Maison Française and the British Empire Building at right toward the heart of the Center—the RCA Building. This is the home of several large corporations, including the National and American Broadcasting systems. In front are the rink and restaurants of the lower plaza. To the left of the plaza, on 49th St., in order from the east, are the Time and Life, Eastern Air Lines, Center Theater and U.S. Rubber buildings. On the right, on 50th St., are, from Fifth Ave., the International, Associated Press, Music Hall and RKO buildings. On 51st St. stands the new Esso Building.

Underground passages connect the structures to which, every work day, 30,000 people come to their offices and 125,000 others come on business or pleasure. Highlights of visitors' tours, starting in the RCA Building, are pictured on following pages. Such trips provide the sightseer with an opportunity to see what manner of city can be built for $59,500,000.

137

The Center's International Building towers above Fifth Avenue and channel between French and British buildings (left foreground).

Rockefeller Plaza, a private street, runs from 48th to 51st Street, past the RCA Building (upper right) and the skating rink which, flying the flags of the United Nations, becomes a dining garden in summer. Skaters may use restaurants close to the ice.

On International Building is a plaque depicting man's history (left). Associated Press Building has Noguchi's steel "News."

Paul Manship's bronze Prometheus looks down on the lower plaza's outdoor restaurant where skaters whirl six months of the year.

This mural, showing the abolition of ancient slavery by the human will, is one of four by Sert in the RCA Building's Great Hall.

Only planned noises go out over the radio network, since the 35 studios are protected from the actual framework of the building by felt-padded steel clips. Each windowless studio is air-conditioned. The technician (above) shows how sound effects are used.

The master control board in the RCA Building is the center of the
National Broadcasting Company's network of 155 stations.

Television broadcasts also originate here. NBC's Studio 8 H, which
is three stories high, seats 1,200 listeners.

Over three acres of roof gardens, largest in the world, thrive in
the Center. This one is six stories up on the British building.

Ezra Winter's "Fountain of Youth" mural in Music Hall's Grand Foyer is 60 feet long. Glass and steel chandelier weighs two tons.

Famed Rockettes pose on the world's largest stage in the world's

largest indoor theater, the Music Hall, which seats 6,200.

Central Park

IF YOU WANT to take a walk around a real Loch, view an ancient Egyptian monument, or give your child a ride in a pony cart, the place to go is Central Park. This large area of woods and rolling hills between Fifth and Eighth avenues is the geographical center of Manhattan.

Central Park actually started when such nineteenth-century New Yorkers as Washington Irving and William Cullen Bryant began agitating for a large "central park" in which citizens could ride, rest and play. Eventually, in 1857, the city purchased acreage for such a park, a tract of scrubland pasture on what was then the northern outskirts of the city. Following the general design laid out at the time, it became the "first real park made in this country."

Central Park today, landscaped throughout and rich in historical associations, offers New Yorkers vacationing at home a variety of recreation. In the shadow of the equestrian statue of General Sherman near the Plaza entrance, top-hatted cabmen in horse-drawn hacks gather to take passengers for leisurely drives through the park. At 64th St. and Fifth Ave. stands the Arsenal, which dates back to 1848 and now serves as headquarters of the city's Park Department. The huge Receiving Reservoir in the center of the park is part of the city's water supply system. Other points of interest are Conservatory Pond, famed for toy yacht regattas; Belvedere Tower, built in 1860 and now a U.S. weather station; and the Obelisk (commonly called Cleopatra's Needle), quarried in Egypt in 1600 B.C.

From Rockefeller Center Observation Roof, the 840 acres of Central Park appear as a rectangular woodland hemmed in by skyscrapers.

A half mile wide, 2½ miles long, the park extends north from the deluxe apartment hotels of West 59th Street to Harlem at 110th.

Landscaped throughout, the park is traversed by 28½ miles of winding footpaths, 9½ miles of automobile roadways. Bridges and arches, 23 of which are named, span its roads and streams. The area is enclosed by rough stone walls with frequent entrance gates.

Typical of the park's irregular terrain is this rock formation in the vicinity of the Plaza entrance at Fifth Avenue and 59th Street. Nearby paths skirt the Pond, sanctuary for wild fowl, and lead north to the Mall, noted for band concerts and folk-dancing.

153

The Mary Harriman Rumsey Playground, one of 22 in the park, has swings, slides, and other recreational facilities for children.

At night the park's seven lakes glitter with reflected light from Manhattan skyscrapers. In summer, New Yorkers come to Central Park to cool off, to promenade around the Reservoir, to dine and dance at the Tavern-on-the-Green overlooking West Drive.

Near the Arsenal and Zoo is a dirt track where children may ride on or behind Shetland ponies. The park offers people of all ages a place to relax; an average of 54,000 visit the grounds each day.

Beyond New Lake (above) is the green oval expanse of Great Lawn.

Young couples, relaxing or walking arm-in-arm, are a common sight.

City horsemen can ride through the park on 5½ miles of bridle path.

Play areas include croquet courts, ball diamonds, skating rinks.

Center of interest at the park Zoo, which occupies a quadrangle near Fifth Avenue and 64th Street, are the sea-lion pool (above) and the monkey house. The Zoo cafeteria is popular for lunch.

For a moderate fee urban sailors may rent flatbottom boats and row on the 72nd Street lake. Soft drinks and light refreshments are served in the boathouse. Fifth Avenue apartments, bordering Central Park on the east, have excellent views the year round.

When cold weather arrives, the park becomes a winter resort, with skiing and sledding on its snow-covered hills, ice-skating on its frozen ponds. The first snowfall of the season brings out the city's photographers to snap pictures of the changed park scene.

Music

ALL THE YEAR round New York tunes up in concert halls and auditoriums to present music in all its forms—from madrigals to swing, from Bach to Benny Goodman. To performer and listener alike, New York is the first city of musical America, with hundreds of recitals and concerts yearly. Good notices from Manhattan's approximately 25 critics mean success for the hopeful making a debut and continued prosperity for the renowned virtuoso.

Some of the city's musical institutions have become bywords for the best in music, among them the Metropolitan Opera and Carnegie Hall. Opera at the Metropolitan is a series of careful productions with the most expensive singers in the world interpreting the dramatic music of three centuries. The Met employs 750 persons, of whom over a hundred are principals and singers, and maintains a wardrobe of 13,000 costumes. Regular performances are attended by an average of 4,000 people, including some 400 standees. Through Saturday afternoon broadcasts, the Metropolitan has become a national institution, bringing opera to an audience of ten million.

Carnegie Hall sponsors concerts by leading symphony orchestras and individual recitalists. From its stage, the Philharmonic broadcasts on Sunday to 13 million people.

Other prominent concert halls are the City Center of Music and Drama, 131 West 55th Street, which presents low-priced ballet, opera, and symphonic concerts; and Town Hall, at 123 West 43rd Street, noted for musical debuts.

163

Society still makes much of the opening of the opera season at the Metropolitan Opera House, between 39th and 40th Streets on Broadway. Operagoers chat during intermission in the foyer (above).

Operas like *Der Rosenkavalier* are staged from November to March.

A ballet troupe performs at the Met in the spring and early fall.

The Met's exterior is dingy brick, but its interior is a glittering

expanse. Lower tiers of boxes form the "Diamond Horseshoe."

Carnegie Hall, completed in 1891 and located at Seventh Ave., and 57th St., is known for big-name recitals and symphony concerts.

The auditorium has excellent acoustics, a seating capacity of 2,760.
The Philharmonic Orchestra plays here from October to April.

Museums

NEW YORK, like Paris, is world famed as a patroness of fine arts. Since its earliest days the city has been one of the cultural centers of the nation, has nurtured and preserved many forms of art. Here artists have come for study, to sell their works, to find encouragement and recognition.

New York's prominence is due in part to the riches collected in its 44 museums. These art, historical and scientific treasures, all easily accessible from mid-Manhattan, offer daily pleasure and enlightenment to resident and visitor, but it is wise to check individual museums for hours and fees.

The Metropolitan Museum of Art (opposite page and pp. 178-181) is one of the art world's showplaces. Sometimes referred to as the "American Louvre," the museum contains works encompassing almost every known school and nationality.

Entire rooms at the Metropolitan are devoted to historical and ancient costumes, to antiquities from Egypt, Cyprus, Greece and Rome. There are rugs from the Near East, a room from a Jain temple, gold cups designed by Benvenuto Cellini and silver tankards fashioned by Paul Revere. The great hall of an eighteenth-century manor house has been reconstructed in the American Wing, which is devoted to decorative arts of the early United States.

Outstanding among the Metropolitan's exhibits is a collection of some 3,000 European and American paintings, including masterpieces by Raphael, Brueghel, Botticelli, Rembrandt, Titian, El Greco, Rubens and Gainsborough. Among modern painters represented are Picasso, Matisse and Van Gogh. Of special note is the museum's collection of oriental art—bronzes, paintings and pottery from China, Japan and India. The Pierpont Morgan Collection of European decorative arts consists largely of early Gothic textiles, furniture and sculpture and 17th-18th century art objects from France. The Bache Collection comprises valuable reliefs, sculpture, paintings and tapestries, all executed before the nineteenth century.

Near the Metropolitan is the Frick Collection (pp. 182-183), which contains the treasures assembled by Henry C. Frick and bequeathed to the public together with the mansion which houses them. In magnificent surroundings, the visitor may study 14th-19th century paintings and view rare enamels, porcelains, bronzes, furniture and rugs. A painting of Philip IV by Velásquez hangs in the Oval Room, and in the East Gallery are works by Vermeer, Cézanne and Ingres. The museum offers free chamber music concerts and lectures on the fine arts.

A visit to the Museum of Modern Art (pp. 174-177) is a change in pace from old to new. Devotees of modern art may keep abreast of trends through the museum's constantly changing exhibitions, may enjoy its permanent collection of such notable European modernists as Gauguin, Degas, Braque, and Americans like Marin, Benton and Calder. The museum exhibits not only modern painting and sculpture, but almost every form of contemporary visual art—photography, motion pictures, architecture and industrial design.

The New York Public Library at 42nd St. and Fifth Avenue has a large picture collection and several rooms devoted to paintings, including two Stuart portraits of Washington. Here, too, is a Print Room containing more than 100,000 items.

The city also has many historical museums. The Museum of the City of New York (pp. 183-184), packed with memorabilia of bygone days, presents a unique album of New York life. Exhibits include a tallyho, an early fire engine and figureheads from sailing ships. Miniature exhibits in glass cases depict scenes from New York's past, and special collections trace the history of communications and the growth of the Stock Exchange.

The New-York Historical Society at 170 Central Park West, founded in 1804, is the second-oldest historical society in the United States. The museum has a notable collection of Americana, a library and collections of silver and paintings.

Outstanding New York scientific museum is the American Museum of Natural History (pp. 186-189). Founded in 1869, it has developed into a vast world of natural science, with 58 exhibit-filled halls occupying 13 acres of floor space, its own carpentry and print shops and power plant. Its treasures, ranging from *Tyrannosaurus rex* to collections of ancient jade and gold, are valued at approximately $30,000,000, represent years of research and scores of expeditions to far-off lands. Some 4,500 persons visit the museum daily.

Natural History Museum tours, described in pamphlets available to visitors, highlight such wonders as 60-million-year-old dinosaur eggs; the Star Ruby and Star Sapphire; the 76-foot-long sulphur-bottom whale; the world's largest frog. Shown here are 150,000 complete specimens of mammals living today. Akeley Memorial Hall of African Mammals presents a cross-section of African animal life in natural settings—gorillas, elephants, lions and other wild animals. In the Hall of the Age of Man are replicas of prehistoric man, including the famous *Pithecanthropus erectus*. The anthropology exhibits cover arts and customs of natives of the world.

Hayden Planetarium (pp. 188-189) presents dramatic displays of the heavens as they are today, were before the Age of Man, and presumably will be a thousand years hence. Exhibits in the Planetarium include an animated model of the solar system and a collection of 3,000 meteorites from outer space.

The Museum of Modern Art, founded in 1929, occupies a five-story building at 11 West 53rd St., is visited by 11,000 persons weekly.

174

The rear façade, constructed chiefly of glass, overlooks the sculpture garden (above), where lunch is served in the summer. The museum has a theater and a film collection tracing the development of the cinema, a library of 13,000 volumes and 11,500 slides.

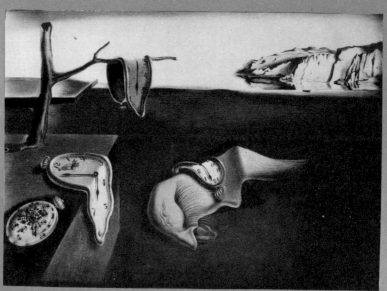

Among the Museum of Modern Art's collection of American and European paintings are *Summer Landscape* (above), by Stuart Davis, and *The Persistence of Memory,* by Salvador Dali.

Other representative paintings include (from left to right) : *Dutch Interior,* by Joan Miro; *Blind Bird,* by Morris Graves; *Self Portrait,* by John Kane; and *Girl Before a Mirror,* by Pablo Picasso.

The Metropolitan Museum of Art, situated in Central Park with its main entrance at Fifth Ave. and 82nd St., was opened to the public in 1880. The original building has had several additions since that time, among them the neo-Greek southwest wing and the central Fifth Avenue section. Museum collections include paintings, sculpture, tapestries, armor, pottery, jewelry, glass and furniture.

In the Roman Peristyle of the Metropolitan, children attend one of the lectures which are part of the museum's education program. Exhibits and lectures are planned to show the close relationship between art and the life of past and present civilizations.

The Metropolitan's Egyptian Collection occupies 15 rooms in the north wing. The wooden statue of a priest in front of his tomb (above) dates from about 2400 B.C. Sculptures on the opposite page, from left to right, represent Queen Hat-shepsut; Seti I making an offering to Osiris; Har-em-hab as a Scribe; Rameses II.

The Frick Collection's Fragonard Room is located in the . . .

Frick Mansion at 1 E. 70th St., which also includes this court.

Paintings are displayed in intimate surroundings in rooms like the Living Hall (above). Over the fireplace is an El Greco, to the right a Holbein. The room also contains a Bellini, two Titians, a statue of Venus by Bologna. Other painters represented in the collection are Rembrandt, Hals, Goya, Whistler and Corot.

The Museum of the City of New York is located in a Georgian
Colonial building at Fifth Ave. and 103rd St. Its galleries present
a panorama of bygone days in New York, with displays of historical portraits and documents, household furnishings and costumes.

The past is recaptured in exhibits like the old New York toy shop.

. . . and the trial of Nathan Hale before General Howe in 1776.

Above is the entrance to Roosevelt Memorial Building of The American Museum of Natural History.

The museum's collection of 800,000 stuffed birds is the largest in the world. The Peruvian Guano Group (above) is in Whitney Hall.

Lifelike habitat groups include such animals as a Siberian tiger, North Asiatic Hall, and a mountain gorilla, Akeley African Hall.

Hayden Planetarium, main entrance at Central Park West and 81st St., is the astronomical hall of the Museum of Natural History.

Under the planetarium dome is the "Theatre of the Skies," where a projection instrument (shown above) reproduces on an artificial sky the sun, moon, planets, fixed stars and Milky Way. Sky shows are given daily, with an explanatory talk before each.

189

Word Mart

WORDS—millions of them each year—are the backbone of one of New York's biggest businesses—the production of books, periodicals and newspapers. For a hundred years publishers have been concentrating in Manhattan, to buy and sell, edit and print words. Today, New York is the largest literary mart in the United States, one of the great publishing centers of the world.

Each day New Yorkers read some 5,500,000 newspapers; there are 56 daily newspapers and periodicals, of which 23 are printed in foreign languages. In tone, the city's newspapers range from tabloid to conservative; in political leaning, from far left to far right. Many of the nation's better-known newspaper columns, by-lined with such names as those of Walter Winchell and Leonard Lyons, originate in New York.

Foremost among Manhattan newspapers is the New York *Times,* whose editions appear on the streets every night between 11 P.M. and 4:30 A.M. Under the management of Adolph S. Ochs, it became famed the world over for foreign news coverage and reliability. Tours of the Times Building may be arranged by telephone for groups who wish to see a metropolitan daily in operation.

New York has been publishing books since its earliest days. Although the city has produced some noted authors, it is much more a writer's market and editorial workshop than a literary center. Many American writers live and work outside New York, visit the city occasionally to make arrangements for the editing and sale of their books. A recent directory of American publishers lists 355 with New York addresses; among them they turn out the major portion of books published in this country. On the scene are some 70 literary agents, middlemen between author and publisher.

A recent offshoot of the publishing business is the book club, distributing published books on a mass scale. Forty of them, including the Book-of-the-Month Club and the Literary Guild, have headquarters in the city. The social life of the book business revolves around authors' luncheons, teas and cocktail parties, given to celebrate the launching of new books and attended by writers, editors, booksellers and agents.

In addition to newspapers and books, New York also publishes magazines. Only memories of the past are such periodicals as the *Century*, the *Bookman* and the *Critic*, which at one time exerted considerable influence on American thought. Today the city produces a large number and variety of magazines—general, women's, literary, news, trade, digest, fashion, pulp and comic. Located in the city are the editorial offices of such well-known magazines as *Collier's*, *Woman's Home Companion*, *Harper's*, *Vogue*, *Life* and *Look*.

Numerous public and special libraries throughout the city are research centers for editors and writers. Leading storehouse for words is the New York Public Library system, second only to the Library of Congress in size, with 144 branches and 4,000,000 borrowers. Some 11,000 people a day visit the Fifth Avenue Central Branch building at 42nd Street, completed in 1911. The greater part of the building is devoted to the reference department, which has 80 miles of bookshelves. The library owns a notable collection of Americana and has a Rare Book Room where a Gutenberg Bible is displayed; its collections of volumes represent more than 3,000 languages and dialects.

Over 3 million printed items are on the reference shelves of the
New York Public Library's Central Branch, Fifth Ave. and 42nd St.

193

Upper East Side

THE UPPER EAST SIDE, New York's area of the "good address," home of the fashionable and wealthy, extends roughly from Fifth Avenue to the East River and north from 47th to 96th Streets. Here, in the world's richest residential district, wealthy and successful New Yorkers maintain apartments and town houses for which they pay the city's highest rents. On the streets, uniformed chauffeurs line up in limousines; housemen exercise pedigreed dogs; nurses in starched caps wheel babies in carriages to the park for a daily airing. Park Avenue, a wide thoroughfare lined with apartment dwellings, is the impressive main artery of the region, and Madison Avenue is its shopping center.

What is now the Upper East Side was rural country when well-to-do New Yorkers started moving uptown from Washington Square in the 1860's. Later, men like Carnegie and Vanderbilt erected mansions on Fifth Avenue, and in 1920 apartment houses began to appear on Park Avenue. Fashionable life today centers in the luxury apartments of the area.

Among the neighborhoods which dot the Upper East Side are Beekman and Sutton Places, which extend for 11 blocks along the East River from 49th to 60th Street. This district is notable for its contrasts of wealth and poverty. Homes of the rich back up to tenements of the poor; underprivileged children play on docks and dead-end streets. Farther north along the East River at East 84th Street, the fashionable residences of Gracie Square adjoin beautiful Carl Schurz Park, a famous Revolutionary site.

195

Park Avenue, from Grand Central to 96th Street, is a rich residential street divided by an enclosed strip of landscaped parking.

Relic of Fifth Avenue's "Millionaires' Row" is this mansion at 79th Street. Marble fronts are now giving way to apartment houses.

Some New Yorkers in high income brackets live above the city's roar in penthouse apartments, cultivate flower and vegetable gardens, may belong to clubs with ballrooms and swimming pools.

The Upper East Side dines out at superb hotels like the Ritz . . .

. . . and congregates for supper dancing at the Plaza.

Hotels

IN NEW YORK'S more than 500 hotels with their 130,000 rooms, a bed for the night can be rented at any price from 20 cents (Bowery flophouse) to $75 (Waldorf-Astoria). At the Waldorf, for that sum, are thrown in such extras as a living room with five tall windows, two or three bedrooms and glittering bathrooms, possibly a bouquet of flowers from the management. The $40,000,000 hotel thus lives up to its past, when at its old site where the Empire State Building now stands it was America's first super-deluxe hotel. It also lives up to its present-day location on Park Avenue between 49th and 50th Streets.

On any one night there may be sleeping under the twin chrome-topped towers in the Waldorf's 2,200 differently priced beds a movie star; two or three foreign diplomats with their staffs, guests of the U.S. Department of State; a king (two were once registered at the same time); the guest who doesn't leave his room all winter; a former President of the United States in his permanent suite; millionaires, salesmen, honeymooners, and a couple of hundred of the more than six million former guests whose likes and dislikes are on file. America's most luxurious hotel has starred in a movie, housed sessions of the Council of Foreign Ministers, has served 3,000 diners a full-course luncheon in 30 minutes.

Also in midtown Manhattan are such large hotels as the New Yorker, Biltmore and the Pennsylvania; the luxury hotels on and near Central Park South and the Plaza: the Pierre, the Plaza, the continental St. Moritz and Hampshire House; the hotels near and on Broadway; and the literary Algonquin.

The Jade Room is one of 25 such halls for entertaining at the Waldorf. Three thousand persons can dine in the Grand Ballroom.

Murals in the Sert Room (above) are by Jose Maria Sert. The Starlight Roof is noted for the quality of its entertainment.

Flowers enliven the main foyer, where tea is served on balconies and guests may watch arrivals from Park Ave. entrance (right).

Shops

MORE THAN three billion dollars are spent each year in New York's 115,000 retail stores, for live turtles, evening gowns, airplanes and other paraphernalia. The plane is available at Macy's, the world's largest store, which is located on Herald Square at 34th Street, at the foot of the Fifth Avenue shopping district and at the top of a wholesale clothing and textile area. Turtles are sold at dozens of pet shops and gowns at scores of salons of varying degrees of splendor; each store has its special appeal. Combined, they make the shopping district one of the city's favorite attractions for visitors.

Most of the principal shops are grouped by type, convenient for comparative shopping, between 34th and 59th streets, and Third and Eighth avenues. In the Herald Square area are Gimbels as well as Macy's ("Does Macy tell Gimbel?") and Saks-34th.

Up Fifth Avenue (page opposite), in the path of the early merchants who expanded the district in this direction over many decades, are the so-called "quality shops" such as Saks-Fifth Avenue, Georg Jensen, Henri Bendel and beauty salons and perfumeries. These stores extend along Madison Avenue as well, and on to 57th and 59th Streets. Art galleries and antique shops also are on 57th near Fifth, and along Third Avenue.

Men's clothing stores like Brooks Brothers and Tripler's are on Madison down to 42nd St. International shops are clustered in Rockefeller Center near Fifth. The windows of some of these stores are shown on following pages.

Fifth Avenue shop windows, with flourishes like this Lord & Taylor

Cinderella tableau, effectively entice shoppers.

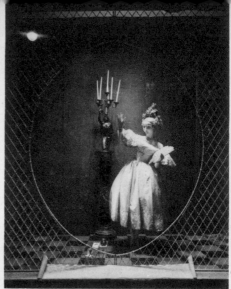

The ballet inspires Bergdorf Goodman's evening dress window
(left). Bonwit Teller uses a ball dress of 1830 to sell perfume.

Abercrombie & Fitch, in the men's shopping district on Madison
Avenue, packs into small space everything a fisherman could want.

Downtown at Herald Square is Macy's, where on an average day 150,000 shoppers swarm in to look at 400,000 separate items. Information clerks among the 11,000 employees answer 25,000 queries a day. At Christmas time daily sales often total a million dollars.

Madison Square Garden

MADISON SQUARE GARDEN, the nation's indoor-sports capital, sells a variety of action. During a midwinter week there may be offered, on successive days, an ice show, a political rally, two basketball games, a rough-and-tumble ice hockey match, an all-star benefit show, a track meet—and, of course, Friday night fights. Then, in season, are the circus (April), the rodeo (September), the Horse Show (November), the Dog Show (February). In Exposition Hall are frequently held the Sportsmen's, Antique, Poultry and Art shows.

The huge building at 8th Ave. and 49th Street, which replaced two earlier Gardens on Madison Square, is giving way to a fourth—the largest ever. The New Garden, on the west side of Columbus Circle from 58th through to 60th Streets, is designed to have 200,000 square feet of floor space for expositions, parking facilities for 2,000 cars, and a stadium with a hockey rink constructed as a waterproof bulkhead deep enough for swimming meets and aquatic shows and with a boxing arena seating 25,000.

The present Garden is the home of professional hockey in New York and of the Rangers hockey team. It is a leading arena for intercollegiate basketball, presenting intersectional games and regional and national tournaments. To provide facilities for such varied activities, brine is pumped through 13 miles of pipe to form an ice rink in seven hours; two hours after a hockey game, tractors will have scraped off the ice and a basketball court will have been set up.

211

The National Horse Show is a highlight of the November schedule.

The large size of the area makes elaborate ice shows possible.

Every spring Ringling Brothers, Barnum & Bailey Circus begins its trek with a month's stand in the Garden, where old and young preview new acts and applaud old ones, such as the aerialists' (above).

To the Garden are invited some of the nation's outstanding college and professional basketball teams. Here the Oklahoma Aggies and Long Island University are competing. The basketball season runs from December through March.

214

Of the five million people who jammed Madison Square Garden in
a recent year, more than half a million came to the hockey games.

The rodeo in October brings 250 cowboys from the cattle states into the Garden—and sometimes practically into the audience's lap.

The competition for titles and for $150,000 in prize money provides fast and thrilling action for city-tied spectators.

Other Points of Interest

BELLEVUE HOSPITAL—This free city hospital, which covers more than 12 city blocks, has a bed capacity of 3,325, admits 62,000 to 70,000 patients a year and treats 2,000 a day in its outpatient clinics, is probably the largest general hospital in the world. It is the oldest in North America, was established on the site of old City Hall in 1736 and moved to its present site—on the East River between 26th and 30th Streets, then Belle Vue Farm —in 1816. Medical care is free to anyone living within the Lower East Side area who cannot afford to pay. It is one of 26 municipal institutions under the city Department of Hospitals. Practically every known disease is treated here, although contagious cases are sent to Willard Parker Hospital nearby.

BRYANT PARK—Behind the New York Public Library's Central Branch at Fifth Ave. and 42nd St. is a small park, where library borrowers read their books outdoors in summer. The park was once the site of the city's Croton Reservoir, its Potter's Field for three years in the 1820's, and the location for the 1853 World's Fair.

CHELSEA—The theater district of the 1880's (on the West Side between 14th and 30th streets) is now a conservative Irish Catholic community. A few old theaters, cafés and hotels remain amid the present-day tenements, apartment houses such as mammoth London Terrace, small shops, pool rooms and seamen's houses. Dr. Clement C. Moore, who wrote "The Night Before Christmas," taught at the General Theological Seminary at 9th Ave. and 20th St. from 1821 to 1850.

COLUMBUS CIRCLE—At the southwest corner of Central Park where Broadway crosses 58th St., at Columbus Circle, the big automobile companies have their offices. The General Motors building on the west side covers an entire block. Sidewalk orators deliver speeches beneath the statue of Columbus in the center of the square.

DAILY NEWS BUILDING LOBBY—In the Daily News Building (see p. 224), the largest revolving globe in the world—12 feet in diameter—is on display in a room lined with maps, charts and clocks giving the time all over the world. The outlines of the continents on the aluminum globe took two months to paint.

F.A.O. SCHWARZ—Rocking horses, slides, model airplanes and toys of every description may be wound up and tried out here. The large toy shop is at 58th St. and Fifth Ave.

FLOWER MARKET—New York's wholesale flower district is centered around Sixth Ave. between 26th and 28th Streets. Millions of flowers, brought in from suburbs or imported from tropical climates, are sold to the retail shops of the city.

FIRST CHURCH OF CHRIST SCIENTIST—This granite church at Central Park West and 96th St. was built in 1903, is notable for its interior marbles and curving staircases.

GILBERT HALL OF SCIENCE—Every kind of mechanical toy, electric train, chemical set and miniature derrick is sold here at Fifth Ave. and 25th St.

GREEK QUARTER—Spiced olives, ikons, Greek maps and shopkeepers sputtering a strange language—Greek to most of us —can be found in the neighborhood of Eighth Ave. and 39th St., where some 50,000 Greeks live. They support themselves as furriers, wholesale cloak and suit dealers and tavern keepers.

MORGAN LIBRARY—This white marble Italian Renaissance building and its annex at Madison and 36th streets contains the J. Pierpont Morgan collection of rare manuscripts and books, one of the finest in the world.

MURRAY HILL — In the days when New York was only a village on the southern tip of Manhattan, Murray Hill was an independent town on a rise of land between what is now 27th and 42nd Streets. As New York spread northward, Murray Hill was absorbed by it and became, in Victorian days, the elite brownstone residential district of the Four Hundred. Some of the homes still stand.

MUSEUM OF NON-OBJECTIVE PAINTING — The Guggenheim Gallery at 24 E. 54th St. is devoted exclusively to the display of new art forms which emphasize design, color, texture and composition rather than resemblance to recognizable objects. A new building is being erected by the museum at 89th St. and Fifth Ave.

NEW YORK MUSEUM OF SCIENCE AND INDUSTRY — The leading museum of its type in the country, in the RCA Building at 30 Rockefeller Plaza, displays new inventions and developments in science. Permanent exhibits include 112 examples of sectional machine parts shown in action; other exhibits are changed frequently to keep up with the news of the day. Visitors may handle the controls of some of the machinery.

NEW YORK SOCIETY LIBRARY — Founded in 1754 and one of the oldest libraries in the country, the New York Society Library has been quartered since 1937 in a mansion at 53 E. 59th St. The library's collections of Americana, fiction and belles-lettres are open to the public for research.

ST. BARTHOLOMEW'S — This wealthy Park Avenue church, next to the Waldorf-Astoria Hotel, is of unusual Byzantine design with round pillared arches and a high dome. It was built in 1930 at a cost of $5,400,000. The three bronze bas-relief front doors are particularly noteworthy.

ST. THOMAS CHURCH — On the northwest corner of Fifth Ave. at 53rd St. is fashionable St. Thomas Protestant Episcopal

Church with its single tower. The interior wood carvings and statuary are notable.

SCHWAB MANSION — This turreted palace on Riverside Drive at 73rd St., former home of steel magnate Charles M. Schwab, is one of the city's unwanted white elephants. Built at a cost of $3,000,000 in 1905, the empty house has 75 rooms, including a chapel and art gallery, is surrounded by a lawn and forbidding iron-grilled fence.

SMITH'S FOLLY — The headquarters of the Colonial Dames of America, set ironically beside a gas station and a garage near the Queensboro Bridge, is a little stone house built in 1799. Surrounded by a lawn and white picket fence, it was originally a stable on the estate of Col. William S. Smith, son-in-law of President John Adams. Smith is believed to have lost it through gambling. It is one of the few remaining historic houses in Yorkville (see below).

"THE LITTLE CHURCH AROUND THE CORNER" — More marriage ceremonies are performed in this pretty little brownstone English chapel between Fifth and Madison on 29th St. than in any other church in the city. Its real name is Church of the Transfiguration (Protestant Episcopal).

YORKVILLE — From Lexington Ave. to the East River between 59th and 96th Streets is the district known as Yorkville, the name of the hamlet established there in the 1790's. Near E. 86th St. is the heart of the German quarter of the city, with its beer gardens and German bands. Czechs, Irish, Hungarians and Slovaks also live in the section.

Midtown Manhattan, with Queens beyond the East River, presents

this impressive night scene. The Chrysler Building is in the center.

The Empire State Building, the world's tallest structure and monument to the boom years, rises 1,250 feet above Fifth Ave., at 34th St. From its towers a 50-mile panorama can be seen.

The *Daily News* (left) and Chrysler buildings are on East 42nd St.

Midtown at 40th (left); N. Y. Hospital-Cornell, 68th St. (right).

The venerable statue of Minerva and the bell ringers has been reinstalled on a new base amidst the crowds in Herald Square.

The Plaza, southern entrance to Central Park, contains the Fountain of Abundance (left) and Saint Gaudens' Statue of Gen. Sherman.

On Riverside Drive stand the Soldiers' and Sailors' Monument (left), at 89th St., and the statue of Joan of Arc, at 93rd St.

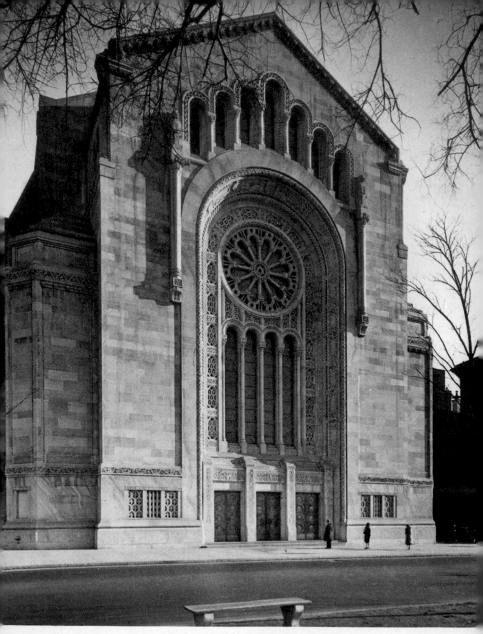

Plain surfaces of the façade of Temple Emanu-El, at 5th Ave. and
65th St., are offset by rich detail and doors with Hebrew symbols.

St. Patrick's Cathedral, with its Gothic Revival spires, occupies the entire block on 5th Ave. at 50th, opposite Rockefeller Center.

The East River slaughterhouse section (above) was cleared to make way for the United Nations headquarters, from 42nd to 48th St.

A familiar street scene south of Times Square is "push boys" frenziedly maneuvering the garment center's output.

Welfare Island, with city hospitals, and Manhattan are seen from
the Queensboro Bridge, which connects the boroughs at 59th St.

Gracie Mansion, in Carl Schurz Park at E. 89th St., was built
in 1799 and restored by the city as a museum-residence in 1927.

Everything from a wooden Indian to an iron lawn bench is available
in the antique, art and curio shops which stretch along Third Ave.
between 42nd and 57th St. Here, forgotten Americana that nobody
wants lies buried next to what may be an antique value.

SECTION C

Upper Manhattan
(above 110th Street)

UPPER MANHATTAN, the island's roof, begins with close-packed dwellings at its southern boundary above Central Park and ends, on the north, with the Harlem River and rustic Inwood Hill Park. Upper Manhattan, the site of several Revolutionary War engagements, contains historical reminders in statues along the Hudson and in houses which have been preserved and opened as museums.

Rivers and efficient bridges are on three sides of the section —the Hudson with the George Washington Bridge on the west; the Harlem with the Henry Hudson, Broadway, University Heights, Washington, Macomb Dam, 145th, 3rd Ave. and Willis Ave. Bridges on the north and east; and the East River and Triborough Bridge on the west. Main U.S. highways leading into the section over these bridges are numbers 9W, 1, 4 and 6 from the west; and 9, 1, 22 and 1A from the north.

The outline map above shows Section C's position in Manhattan. As in other sections of this book, the stories on the following pages are numbered to correspond with black-circled numbers that locate them on the Section C map (opposite). On pages 264-275 are pictures and text describing additional points of interest in this section.

Harlem

THERE is not one Harlem, but three, crowded into the area above Central Park that extends on the west from Morningside and St. Nicholas Avenues east and north to the East and Harlem Rivers and 155th St. And there are two sides to Negro Harlem, which lies above the other two: the district of hot music and acrobatic dancing pictured on the opposite page, and a quiet, residential Harlem housing half a million Negroes.

Spanish Harlem, centered just above the Park, is a home for many Latin-Americans—mainly Puerto Ricans driven to the city by poverty after the first World War. In business places between 110th and 116th Streets, native foods such as Andalusian stew, and Spanish records and musical instruments are displayed. The large Public Market Place, along Park Avenue, reflects the district's foreign flavor in such offerings as tropical fruits, dried red peppers, spices and fish. Catholic churches are important in the life of this area.

Jam-packed Italian Harlem, overlooking Ward's and Randall's Islands in the East River and Triborough Bridge, drew its immigrants largely from Sicily and southern Italy. Here, too, markets indicate old-world tastes in macaroni, olive oils, devilfish, razor clams, pomegranates and garlic; restaurants serve minestrone, chicken cacciatore and pizza pie. The fiesta of Our Lady of Mount Carmel is celebrated with an elaborate parade in July from the religious center of the district, the church of the same name on E. 115th St.

Negro Harlem represents the highest and the lowest status attained by the Negro in the North. Overcrowded, overpriced tenements with attendant vice, disease and delinquency, in "the Valley" east of 7th Ave., contrast with more affluent housing on Sugar Hill, to the north, where the successful live with dignity. Noisy honkytonks on Lenox Avenue are far removed from the quiet apartments of the professional class in "the Golden Edge," overlooking Central Park.

Religion, which plays an important role in Harlem, has its highly publicized and relatively unknown aspects. The Holy Rollers, the Negro Synagogue, Father Divine and his thousands of followers with names like Heavenly Dove and Glorious Illumination have been described extensively. Not so well known are the 150 more sober churches such as Methodist Mount Calvary, Catholic St. Aloysius and, foremost, the Abyssinian Baptist Church at 132 W. 138th St., an imposing structure built of New York blue stone.

Night life in Harlem does not consist exclusively of jitterbugging at the Savoy or at Small's cabaret on Seventh Avenue. The Young Men's Christian Association at 180 W. 135th St. offers a cultural program of a different sort. The New York Public Library branch at 103 W. 135th St. houses the Schomburg collections of several thousand volumes on the Negro. In Harlem have lived and work such well-known craftsmen as Countee Cullen, Langston Hughes, Claude McKay and James Weldon Johnson, writers; Aaron Douglas and E. Sims Campbell, artists; actor Richard B. Harrison, "De Lawd" of "The Green Pastures"; and such musical leaders as Duke Ellington and Fletcher Henderson. Dancer Bill Robinson and fighter Joe Louis have occupied important places in Harlem.

Many of the district's slums are made up of former mansions built in days when the area was, first, a district of country estates and, later, a site of fashionable residences. Soon after 1900 Negroes began to move in when a real estate boom exploded there. More Negroes emigrated during the first World War from the South and the West Indies. Some aspects of Negro Harlem are pictured in the following pages.

A hero of Harlem—and of many American sports fans—opened this eating place at 11 W. 125th St.

125th Street, shown looking east from Eighth Ave., is Harlem's main business street. At left is the noted Apollo Theater.

Harlem's eating places offer a variety of fare, but favorite foods are barbecued spareribs and chicken prepared like this.

Celebrated Negro bands play at the Savoy Ballroom, Lenox Ave. and 140th St., home of the Lindy Hop, Truckin' and the Susie Q.

Skillful Negro comedians and dancers appear with good musicians at the Apollo Theater, Harlem's "opera house."

Harlem's half million residents live in housing designed to accommodate 75,000. The over-crowding results in slums like this.

One solution of the housing problem is suggested by developments like Harlem River Houses and Laurence Dunbar Apartments.

IN MEMORY OF
ROBERT GOELET
CLASS OF 1860

ALMA MATER

Universities

NEW YORK'S vast educational plant, from nursery schools through graduate colleges, reflects its quick-paced, multi-peopled environment. The size of the city is mirrored in the huge annual enrollment figures of New York University (57,000) (see page 319), Columbia University (38,000) and the four colleges of the City of New York (65,000). The latter, administered by the Board of Higher Education, includes six campuses, scattered for the convenience of students through the expansive metropolitan area. The city's skyscrapers are echoed, too, in the 16-story building housing Hunter College, at 68th Street and Park Avenue; and the 16-story John Jay Hall at Columbia University.

The main campuses of two of these schools, as well as several other important educational institutions, are located in Upper Manhattan. Columbia is on Morningside Heights at 116th Street and Broadway, City College on Amsterdam Avenue from 136th to 140th Streets.

Columbia, one of the world's great endowed universities, contributed scientists to early atomic research; the military significance of such work was demonstrated in 1939. Among its noted alumni and teachers have been government figures such as Rexford G. Tugwell, A. A. Berle, Jr., and Raymond Moley; educator John Dewey, exponent of the philosophy of practice and experiment; historians David S. Muzzey, Charles A. Beard and James Harvey Robinson; Prof. Harold C. Urey, noted for his work with "heavy water" and atomic energy; Chief Justices Charles Evans Hughes and Harlan Fiske Stone. The university was founded in 1754 as King's College; during the Revolutionary

245

War its building, then downtown, was requisitioned by the British. During its slow growth it acquired the land, which it still owns, where Rockefeller Center now stands (see page 137). Now it houses on Morningside Heights its liberal arts college and its schools of medicine, law, dentistry, optometry, architecture, business, engineering, political science, library service, journalism and philosophy. Its campus is a series of closed courts about the domed central edifice, Low Memorial Library. Other units include Barnard, for women; and teachers and medical schools.

City College, born in 1847, is one of the four units of the Colleges of the City of New York. (Others: Hunter, Brooklyn, and Queens Colleges.) City College has its main buildings, of late English Gothic design, arranged on a quadrangle, above Amsterdam Avenue. The massive Main Building overlooks St. Nicholas Park. Liberal arts and sciences, technology and education are taught here. The School of Business and Civic Administration is at Lexington Avenue and 23rd Street.

Nearby, on the grounds of the Society of the Sacred Heart, a Roman Catholic order, extending from Convent Avenue to St. Nicholas Terrace, from 130th to 135th Streets, are the buildings of the Father Young Memorial High School, the Annunciation Girls' School and Manhattanville College, founded in 1841 as a college for women. North of Barnard College, from 120th to 122nd Streets, are the buildings of the Union Theological Seminary arranged like an English college quadrangle. The seminary, more than 100 years old and now affiliated with Columbia, is noted for the ministers and missionaries it has graduated. Across Broadway, at 122nd Street, is the Jewish Theological Seminary of America, housed in buildings of Colonial Georgian design, including a library of rare books and manuscripts. Still further north, on Claremont Avenue, is the famous Juilliard School of Music whose buildings have restrained classical-modern lines.

At 192nd Street and Audubon Avenue is the George Washington High School, an excellent example of New York's 733 public schools in which 33,000 teachers instruct 850,000 pupils.

The statue of Alma Mater shown on the previous page is in front
of the Columbia Library, which contains 1,615,000 books.

At Barnard College, for women, a part of Columbia University, students use this pleasant walk from Barnard Hall to Brooks (rear).

This modified Gothic archway frames the massive main building of City College, at the western end of the campus on Amsterdam Avenue. The college's buildings cost $4,000,000 when they were erected, 1903-07. Manhattan schist from a subway excavation was used, with a trim of white terra cotta. Nearby is the school's Lewisohn Stadium, famous for summer concerts.

Riverside Church   .

NEW YORK'S 3,181 places of worship, many of architectural beauty and historical significance, attest to the city's long tradition of religious tolerance. Today's 4,245,907 church members include followers of almost every known faith; church property is valued at about $286,000,000.

Churches offering spiritual rest are scattered through every borough. Two of Manhattan's best-known Protestant churches, for example, are Riverside and the Cathedral of St. John the Divine. Uptown at Riverside Drive and 122nd Street the magnificent edifice of Riverside Church commands the Hudson River. The church, nominally Baptist but offering fellowship to members of all denominations, was endowed by the Rockefellers and is linked with the name of Dr. Harry Emerson Fosdick, its longtime pastor. In addition to regular services, Riverside Church sponsors a variety of community activities.

Some aspects of the Gothic structure, for which the thirteenth-century Cathedral of Chartres furnished architectural inspiration, are shown on the following pages. The church proper seats 2,500 persons; its stained glass windows are among the finest in the city. The church tower (opposite page) contains a 72-bell carillon.

The massive stone buildings of the Cathedral of St. John the Divine (Protestant Episcopal), main entrance at Amsterdam and 112th, occupy 11½ acres overlooking Morningside Heights. In process of construction for over half a century, the completed cathedral will be the largest church building in America, with a seating capacity of 15,000 and standing room for 40,000.

Riverside Church's vaulted nave is 215 feet long, 100 feet high.

Prophets at left of main doorway (left), a grotesque (right) . . .

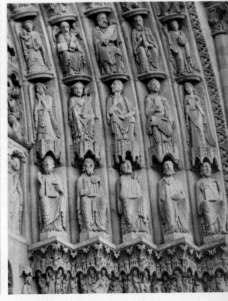

a gargoyle (left), tympanum's arches (right) are typical details.

Historic Houses

ALTHOUGH THE FACT is frequently overlooked, a number of historically important houses still stand in New York City. For example, the Jumel Mansion (opposite page) was used as headquarters by General Washington and, later, by the British command after American forces were defeated in important Revolutionary War encounters in upper Manhattan.

In the battle of Harlem Heights, Sept. 16, 1776, the Americans, who had retreated from Long Island, forced the British to move to a buckwheat field where Barnard College now stands at 116th Street, and then on to what is now 105th Street, where reinforcements joined the Redcoats. On Nov. 16 the American garrison at Fort Washington, at about 183rd Street, was attacked on three sides and fired upon by warships from the Hudson. The Americans were forced to surrender. Present-day Fort Tryon Park includes the site of Fort Washington.

A Royalist sympathizer, Roger Morris, built the Jumel Mansion in 1765, which now stands in the park named for him at 160th Street. He occupied the house until he went back to England in 1775. Other famous names are linked with this Georgian Colonial structure. Stephen Jumel, a French merchant, in 1810 purchased the property which at one time extended from river to river with "Fishing, Oystering and Clamming at either end." After Jumel's death in 1832, Aaron Burr, then 80, married his widow and moved into the mansion. It is now owned by the city, which operates it as a museum open to the public.

255

A statue of Alexander Hamilton at 287 Convent Avenue stands in front of the Grange which he built in 1802 in post-Colonial style as a country place. The two-story frame structure, now wedged between St. Luke's Church and apartments, is open to the public.

Claremont Inn, manor house built in 1783, sheltered many historical figures, now is a restaurant on Riverside Drive.

The city's only eighteenth-century farmhouse, the Dyckman House at 204th St. and Broadway, was restored after the Revolution.

The Cloisters

A VISIT to the medieval Cloisters, a massive building rising impressively from rocky ledges on the northern heights of Fort Tryon Park, is a step back to the Middle Ages. Within the walls of the Cloisters, the devout atmosphere of twelfth to fifteenth century ecclesiastical life has been recreated; the building, a museum piece itself, and the art objects it contains constitute the world's finest collection of Romanesque and Gothic religious relics.

Donated by John D. Rockefeller, Jr., the Cloisters, part of the Metropolitan Museum of Art (see p. 170) were opened as a public museum in 1938. The building incorporates the remains of five European cloisters where monks once walked and meditated; a Romanesque chapel and a variety of ancient stonework, doorways and stained glass. To complete the old-world scene are plantings of yew, myrtle and ivy in the various gardens, plotted from details in ancient manuscripts, paintings and tapestries.

Shown on the opposite page are the arcades and garden court of the Cuxa Cloister, central and largest section of the museum. This cloister, originally part of the French abbey of Saint-Michel-de-Cuxa, was built in the twelfth century when this abbey was celebrated throughout western Europe.

Most renowned of the Cloisters' treasures is the series of six tapestries depicting the allegorical Hunt of the Unicorn. Other great works of art include a twelfth-century Spanish crucifix, the tomb effigy of Jean d'Alluye, a 15th-century ceiling from Illescas, and the sculptured Lion from Zamora.

The Cloisters, dominated by a square tower (above), is built of granite in the form of a series of rambling medieval monasteries.

Twelfth-century monks assembled for business of the day under the
arches of the Pontaut chapter house, which forms an integral part
of the Cloisters. Also incorporated as sections of the building are
the Bonnefont and Trie cloisters and the Froville Arcade.

Panel detail above, part of a sepulchral monument built about 1300, represents the funeral rites of Armengol VII, Count of Urgel.

Halls of the Cloisters contain such notable sculptures as this 15th
century head of Christ, and many statues of the Virgin.

Other Points of Interest

AMERICAN ACADEMY OF ARTS AND LETTERS—Outstanding men of letters who have attained membership in this society have contributed to its collection of paintings and manuscripts. Some of the finest examples of American art, music and literature are on exhibit here. The Academy building is in the Washington Heights museum group at Broadway and 156th St.

AMERICAN GEOGRAPHICAL SOCIETY—Maps and atlases of every description—comprising one of the largest collections in the Western Hemisphere—may be seen in the library of the American Geographical Society on Washington Heights at 156th St.

AMERICAN NUMISMATIC SOCIETY—Collectors of coins will find rare pieces from 700 B.C. to the present day in the display cases of the American Numismatic Society on Washington Heights. Emphasis is on rare coins of the United States, but unusual pieces from every country in the world are included.

BAKER FIELD—Columbia University's football stadium, baseball field, cinder track and boathouses are located at 218th St. and Broadway on the Harlem River.

FORT TRYON PARK—Atop the highest point in New York, north of the George Washington Bridge, is a 62-acre landscaped plateau on the site of Old Fort Tryon, which figured in the Revolution. In all directions there is a magnificent view from observation terraces and parking spaces. The park has several miles of shaded walks and two miles of roads.

GRAVE OF AN AMIABLE CHILD — St. Clair Pollock was drowned at the age of five, on July 15, 1797, near what is now Riverside Drive and the Claremont Inn. His uncle erected an iron grating around the grave and a stone urn with the inscription, "Erected to the Memory of an Amiable Child," which still stand here.

GROTTO OF NOTRE DAME DE LOURDES — The vaulted apse of this French Renaissance Church on Morningside Drive at 114th St. appears to have been carved from the rock of Morningside Cliff. Sermons are entirely in French.

HARLEM RIVER SHIP CANAL — The narrow thread of Spuyten Duyvil Creek was enlarged in 1895 into the Harlem River Ship Canal. The channel, now 400 feet wide, facilitates passage from the upper end of the Harlem into the Hudson.

HENRY HUDSON PARKWAY — The Henry Hudson Parkway begins at 72nd St. as an extension of the West Side Express Highway and extends to the Saw Mill River Parkway at the Westchester County line. Up to the George Washington Bridge it parallels Riverside Drive through a park section developed with fountains, playgrounds and football fields on reclaimed land along the river. It loops under the Bridge and follows the base of the steep cliffs on the other side which are topped by Fort Tryon Park and the Cloisters. Finally it cuts across Inwood Park to the toll stop at the Henry Hudson Bridge, which takes it out of Manhattan.

HIGH BRIDGE — Built in 1837 at Amsterdam Ave. and 173rd St., High Bridge is part of the New York water supply system, bringing water to Manhattan from up-state. Original stone piers in the Harlem River bed were replaced by a steel span in the 1920's, but many of the old bridge's arches remain today. The High Bridge Water Tower stands at the Manhattan side of the bridge.

INWOOD HILL PARK—In the far northwest corner of Manhattan, where the island narrows and the Harlem River turns into the Hudson, is a high piece of woodland where berries, pines and maples grow as wild as when Henry Hudson visited the Algonquin Indian settlement there. Indian caves, relics, including a rock dwelling complete with tools and pottery, and Revolutionary war mementoes have been uncovered. The park is crossed by the Henry Hudson Parkway.

ISHAM PARK—The 20-acre park, site of the old Isham homestead, overlooks the Harlem River and adjoins Inwood Hill Park on 207th St. west of Broadway.

LEWISOHN STADIUM—Best known for the outdoor concerts given here at popular prices by the Philharmonic Symphony Orchestra on summer evenings, the stadium is also the athletic arena for C.C.N.Y. It is located on the City College campus at 136th St. and Amsterdam Ave.

MOTHER CABRINI HIGH SCHOOL—The body of Mother Frances Xavier Cabrini, the first United States citizen to be canonized by the Roman Catholic Church (July, 1946), is entombed in the chapel. The school is a modern brick structure at 701 Fort Washington Ave.

MUSEUM OF THE AMERICAN INDIAN—Canoes, totem poles, tepees, arrowheads and every kind of instrument used by every kind of American Indian from Eskimo to Inca are on display in the Heye Foundation Museum at Washington Heights.

POLO GROUNDS—Home of the New York Giants at 155th St. and 8th Ave. overlooking the Harlem River, the Polo Grounds stadium has a seating capacity of 67,000, is used for big league football and baseball games.

SCHURZ STATUE—At Morningside Drive and 116th St. is a statue of the liberal editor of the N.Y. *Evening Post* for many years, Carl Schurz, a German-American immigrant.

ST. ANN'S CHURCH FOR DEAF MUTES—The structure occupied by this Episcopal church, first of its kind in the world, was built in 1892. The chapel is brightly lit during services so that the congregation may "read" the sermon delivered in sign-language.

TILDEN STATUE—Governor of New York and Democratic nominee for President in 1876, Samuel J. Tilden is memorialized in a nine-foot statue at 112th St. and Riverside Drive.

TRIBOROUGH STADIUM—On the lower end of Randall's Island, where the three arms of the Triborough Bridge meet, is a municipal stadium with one of the largest movable outdoor stages in the world. Seating capacity is almost 30,000.

TRINITY CHURCH CEMETERY—The largest cemetery on Manhattan, extending from Riverside Drive to Amsterdam Ave., and from 153rd to 155th Streets, is a part of Trinity Church downtown, at Wall St. and Broadway. The cemetery's Chapel of the Intercession (see p. 272) is one of eight in Trinity Parish. The son of Charles Dickens, the novelist; Audubon, the naturalist; and other famous personages are buried in this quiet graveyard bisected by upper Broadway.

U.S.S. PRAIRIE STATE—This decommissioned battleship, anchored at the foot of 136th St., is used for training purposes by the U.S. Naval Reserve. The ship was formerly the *U.S.S. Illinois.*

YESHIVA UNIVERSITY—The oldest Jewish university in the Western Hemisphere (founded in 1897), this school includes a Talmudical academy, Yeshiva College, a theological seminary for the training of Orthodox rabbis, a teachers' institute, a graduate school, a school of higher Jewish studies and an institute of mathematics. It is located at Amsterdam Ave. and 187th St.

Overlooking the Hudson, Grant's Tomb stands in an oval on Riverside Drive at 123rd St.

Across the Drive is International House, 40 per cent of whose residents, including these Indian students, come from foreign lands.

Nestling almost unnoticed under the gigantic George Washington
Bridge at 179th St. is this lighthouse commanding the Hudson.

Great apartment houses are perched above the West Side Highway and the Hudson River, such as Castle Village (above) at 183rd St.

Adding to the beauties of Riverside Drive is this rotunda at a clover-leaf, with its lighted fountain (above).

The remains of Architect Bertram Goodhue and this typical Gothic detail are in Trinity's Chapel of the Intercession, at 155th St.

Lofty piers in the nave further the Gothic design of the Episcopal
Cathedral of St. John the Divine, at Amsterdam Ave. and 112th St.

Five museums in the Washington Heights group face Broadway at
155th St. The Hispanic Society of America, for study of Portuguese
and Spanish culture, erected the statue of *El Cid* (above), Spanish
hero, in its court. The Academy of Arts and Letters is also here.

The massive pile of the Columbia-Presbyterian Medical Center, one of the world's great medical capitals, is located along Broadway from 165th to 168th Sts. It is noted for research in such problems as eye cornea transplants, and for its schools and clinics.

SECTION D

The Boroughs
and Environs

THIS SECTION covers the four boroughs (other than Manhattan) that make up Metropolitan New York, and includes some of the highlights of neighboring districts. The outline map above and the air photo-map on opposite page show the boroughs' encircling relationship to Manhattan. The stories on following pages are numbered; corresponding numerals are shown on the large foldout map in the front of the book, to aid in locating stories. On pages 346-359 are pictures and text describing additional points of interest in this section.

Every modern method of transport is available to carry borough residents, commuters and out-of-town visitors from or through this section to jobs or vacations in Manhattan. (See the story on transportation, pages 362-375.) This section is the home of nine million people; their dwellings, as indicated in the following pages, range from one-room apartments to Long Island and Westchester estates complete with swimming pools. It also contains notable beaches, manufacturing establishments, zoos and historical buildings.

All visitors to the metropolis pass through or over some part of this section.

Brooklyn

A STRANGE SIGHT greeted American soldiers as they strolled for the first time down the Champs Elysées after the recapture of Paris. It was a huge sign, erected by a Brooklyn department store, which shouted greetings from "the land of the Dodgers."

For such exuberant displays of its colorful civic personality Brooklyn is known throughout the world. The borough's more fantastic facets have crept into newspapers, magazines, movies, radio and conversation until today there are few people who have not heard of Coney Island or "dem bums."

However, the prosaic statistics of Brooklyn are indeed amazing. For example, within its 71 square miles, approximately 3,000,000 people have their homes, almost as many as live in Chicago, giving rise to the appelation "bedroom of New York." With the exception of its waterfront and downtown shopping and business districts, the borough (seen in foreground, opposite page) is devoted almost exclusively to residential communities, many of which retain the names they had when still separate villages not yet gobbled up in Brooklyn's expansion. Ask a Brooklynite where he lives and his answer will undoubtedly be "Brownsville," "Flatbush," "Bensonhurst," or one of the other 25 subdivisions.

Until 1898, when Brooklyn became part of New York City proper, it had been for 64 years a separate city. Once the merger occurred, the Williamsburg and Manhattan bridges were quickly thrown across the East River and, with the already erected Brooklyn Bridge, opened new connecting links between Brooklyn and

Manhattan. With the completion of subway and auto tunnels beneath the river, the union was firmly cemented.

Brooklyn's 33 miles of improved waterfront are responsible for the clearance of about 40 percent of New York's foreign commerce, its facilities including 14 trunk railways, 70 steamship freight lines and huge shipping warehouses. The borough is also an important manufacturing center.

Sectionally, Brooklyn can be classified as Downtown, North, West, East and Middle. Downtown Brooklyn contains business, recreational, governmental and educational establishments; North Brooklyn, its greatest concentration of slum areas and also the huge 25-acre Williamsburg Housing Project; West Brooklyn, its old residential sections, stretching to a junction with newer port facilities; East Brooklyn, which contains modern residences on the site of Long Island's earliest communities; and Middle Brooklyn, which is almost entirely free of industrial enterprise and embraces Prospect Park.

Lying as it does at the western tip of Long Island, Brooklyn is within easy driving distance of many recreational areas mentioned elsewhere in this volume. Among its own playgrounds, Prospect Park, Coney Island (p. 294), Sheepshead Bay and Ebbets Field (p. 288) are best known. Cultural activities in Brooklyn center about its museums, libraries, schools and the Academy of Music. Its profusion of churches of all denominations has earned Brooklyn the title of "Borough of Churches."

Despite its air of clowning, its own peculiar jargon—"Brooklynese"—the city emerges as a responsible and respectable member of the sisterhood of boroughs that is New York.

Fulton Street (above), known as "department store row," is Brooklyn's oldest thoroughfare and busiest downtown shopping street.

Kings Highway, where the Flatlands Dutch Reformed Church stands, was the scene of Cornwallis' flanking movement against the Americans during the Battle of Long Island in 1776. In the grave-yard members of New York's oldest Dutch families are interred.

A statue of Henry Ward Beecher, whose fiery anti-slavery sermons shook the nation, overlooks the yard of Plymouth Church, Brooklyn.

Brooklyn Museum (left), on Eastern Parkway, is close to Prospect Park's entrance, framed by Soldiers' and Sailors' Memorial Arch.

One of four municipal colleges offering free tuition to New York City residents is Brooklyn College (above), which opened in 1937.

At the junction of Flatbush Avenue and Eastern Parkway, opposite Prospect Park, is the neo-classic Brooklyn Public Library (above).

285

Eastern Parkway is one of several Brooklyn residential districts whose homes still display antiquated round facades and high stoops.

Bay Ridge is one of Brooklyn's most spacious residential sections. Homes along Shore Road (above) face the Narrows and Upper Bay.

Good food, fishing, horse and auto racing made Sheepshead Bay a sporting mecca until 1919. Today, only the food and fish remain.

In Brooklyn, no event on any sporting calendar takes precedence

over an Ebbets Field meeting of the Dodgers and New York Giants.

U.S. Navy Yard

RESIDENTS OF BROOKLYN probably will blink at the term "New York Naval Shipyard," yet that is the official designation for their own familiar Brooklyn Navy Yard.

Clustered in the crook of the Wallabout Bay elbow in the East River, near the Brooklyn anchor of Manhattan Bridge, the Yard has spread from the original 42 acres purchased by the government in 1801 to its present 290 acres, exclusive of a vast annex at Bayonne, N.J., across the Upper Bay. However, the immensity of the world's largest navy yard can best be grasped by considering its capacities. Just prior to V-J Day, the Yard was employing 69,000 workers as compared to the World War I peak of 8,700. Carrying out its function of building and repairing fighting and merchant marine vessels in the New York area, during a recent year the Yard serviced 1,616 ships and made 7,286 service calls to ships in the harbor. A record was set in October, 1944, when 40 destroyer escorts, 24 destroyers, two cruisers and the battleship, *U.S.S. Texas,* were laid up in its confines.

The Yard has played a prominent part in history since Revolutionary Days, when the Battle of Long Island was waged nearby. Among the more famous vessels built or launched at the Yard were the *Fulton, Halstead's Folly,* an early, cigar-shaped submarine still on exhibition, the *U.S.S. Maine* of Spanish-American War fame and the 45,000-ton aircraft carrier, *Franklin D. Roosevelt.*

Although the Yard is steadily busy with repair and maintenance work on active ships, it is prepared and equipped to fill its key spot in America's national defense network.

Lying along the Brooklyn shore between Manhattan and Williamsburg bridges is the enormous building and repair plant of the New

York Naval Shipyard. In drydocks shown above, which range in size from 326 to 700 feet, ships of *U.S.S. Missouri* class were built.

Coney Island

FEW EUROPEAN VISITORS realize it, but as they approach New York's harbor, their first glimpse of the United States is of Coney Island, one of the city's favorite playgrounds. As land is neared, the tower of the Half Moon Hotel slowly emerges from the horizon which is Long Island, followed by a Ferris wheel and a tank of the Brooklyn Borough Gas Company. John de Verazzano and Henry Hudson, early explorers of the American continent, also peered at Coney in their search for a Northwest Passage to Cathay, but at that time it was a rabbit-infested island off the Brooklyn shore.

Today, no longer an island and cleared of rabbits, Coney has a winter population of 60,000, a summer population of 150,-000 and more than 35,000,000 visitors each year. On a hot summer Sunday, more than a million bathers pack its sandy beach seeking escape from city heat.

A two-mile boardwalk connects Sea Gate and Brighton Beach, between which communities lies Coney Island. On either side of this boardwalk are explanations for Coney's universal fame—the Atlantic Ocean and an amusement park unexcelled elsewhere. Behind bathhouses that line the boardwalk is a hodgepodge of roller-coasters, Loop-o-planes, Virginia Reels, Whips, baby incubators, wax works, side shows, and sidewalk stands which sell frosted custard, malted milk, seafood, corn-on-the-cob, sugar cotton candy, taffy, jelly apples, French fried potatoes, hot dogs, soft drinks and beer. To this topsy-turvy land comes a daily stream of spectators, by bus, subway, trolley and automobile.

Many Coney visitors insist on riding the whirling Virginia Reel, or gazing seaward from the Ferris wheel's cabooses (background).

Much of the Midway's hub-bub and commotion emanates from
Coney Island's many freak shows Barkers rattle off their spiels with
the rapidity of tobacco auctioneers and, with the visual aid of
scantily dressed performers, repeatedly lure ever-curious crowds.

297

For all its attractions, Coney's biggest show is still the crowd. Children's faces as they eat corn-on-the-cob or ice cream sticks . . .

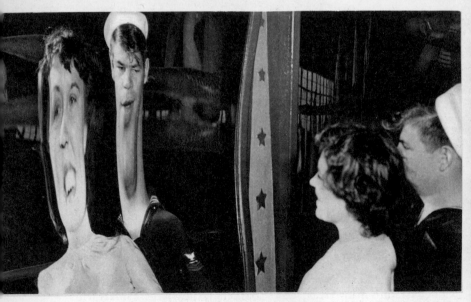

. . . and the distorted facial expressions which look out from "funny mirrors" are all part of the continuous fun festival.

Yet, on really stifling days, the big show takes place along the jammed beaches, where every variety of beachwear is represented.

Concessionaires and police can expect at least a million visitors at Coney on a hot summer Sunday. From every section of the city

perspiring New Yorkers descend upon and spread over the beach
with such early morning speed as to obscure the sands.

Staten Island

THE BOROUGH OF RICHMOND—like three of the other four boroughs—is an island. (Only the Bronx is on the mainland.) But there Richmond's resemblance to the remainder of the city ceases. Located five miles south across the Upper Bay from Manhattan's tip, Staten Island, which is Richmond, has no vaulting bridges or speedy subways to connect it with the metropolis. Instead, it relies on its historic ferry service (see page 40), instituted with sailboats soon after the Revolutionary War. For this reason Staten Island has an isolated air of rural peace and quiet ways which contrast sharply with the bustle of other boroughs.

The pear-shaped island, with an area of 57 square miles, nearly twice that of Manhattan, has a population of only 180,000. Many of these residents take the ferry five or six mornings a week to Manhattan and return eagerly each evening, because five minutes after docking at industrial St. George (opposite page), they can substitute rural for urban living. True, shipways and factories sprawl along the east shore and the northern area washed by the Kill Van Kull, opposite industrial Jersey. But the real Staten Island lies a short distance inland, its backbone a range of hills continuing from St. George down to La Tourette Park, broken by two parks and the zoo in Clove Valley. Topping the ridge is Todt Hill, 409 feet high, the highest point of land south of Maine on the Atlantic coast. Sprinkled over the island, on the few main roads, are communities that exhibited a potent individualism decades before the island became a part of Greater New York in 1898. Even today the residents, 58 per cent of whom own their own homes, are inclined to claim allegiance to, say, Dongan

Hills, New Dorp, Huguenot or Pleasant Plains, which are scattered on or near Richmond Road as it stretches to the foot of the island and Tottenville, rather than to the overall City of New York.

Farms are laid out on flat reaches to the south and on side roads. History hangs over these areas and has left visible reminders, some of which are pictured on following pages. Indians wiped out three settlements before colonization succeeded; the Dutch bought the land five separate times from the redskins. The British took the island at the beginning of the Revolutionary War, and their troops repulsed the Americans at St. George. During the Civil War it was an asylum for the wives of Southern planters.

Cannonballs and arrowheads are still dug up by local antiquarians on old battlegrounds, and mementoes are to be found at St. George in the Staten Island Museum, the borough's cultural center. Models reproduce an Indian attack; marine life and natural history are shown in exhibits and historical papers.

Other reminders of wars ancient and more recent are to be found at Fort Wadsworth, protecting the Narrows where the British fired the last shot of the Revolutionary War, and at 383-acre Halloran General Hospital, in the Willowbrook area south of St. George, where the U.S. Army and later the Veterans Administration cared for hundreds of thousands of men wounded in World War II.

The island is the birthplace of Alan Seeger, who wrote his prophetic "I Have a Rendezvous with Death" during the first World War. Famous residents, attracted by beaches and the pastoral scene, included James Russell Lowell, prima donnas Jenny Lind and Adelina Patti, Edwin Markham, author of "The Man with the Hoe," and Giuseppe Garibaldi, the Italian patriot, who lived here in exile from his native land.

This Pleasant Plains farm suggests Staten Island's rural charm.

The bridge to Bayonne, N.J., indicates the island's industrialism.

Through the bronze doors of this million-dollar mausoleum in the Moravian Church's Cemetery at New Dorp were carried the remains of most of the Vanderbilt family, including Commodore Cornelius, who ran a ferry service—by sailboat—to Manhattan.

The Church of St. Andrew, at La Tourette Park, chartered by Queen Anne in 1713, was rebuilt with its original walls.

Staten Island's historic structures include the Christopher House, where secret meetings were held during the Revolution.

The Dutch frame Vorleezers House, 63 Arthur Kill Road, is America's oldest elementary school building, the island's first church.

British and American delegates met at the Billopp House, at the foot of the island, in a futile attempt to end the Revolution.

The main wing of the Austen House, which overlooks the Narrows, was built before 1669. Unevenly spaced dormers were added later.

The Bronx

THE BRONX, borough of apartment houses, is the only part of New York City connected with the mainland. But despite its land-attached position, the Bronx, like other boroughs, is bounded by water. Situated above the fork of the East and Harlem rivers, touched on the upper western end by the Hudson and by Long Island Sound among the islands off its eastern shore, the Bronx actually has an 80-mile waterfront. Inland, the Hutchinson and Bronx Rivers traverse its northeast and central sections.

Three main ridges, however, final outcroppings of the Berkshires and the Green Mountains, give the Bronx is most widely-known characteristic—hilliness. In fact, derisive persons from other boroughs usually place the Bronx in the foothills of the Adirondacks—a designation which at once scores its hilly nature and its place as northernmost arm of the city.

From the time Jonas Bronk first settled his 500 acres of land in the borough until the mid-nineteenth century, the Bronx remained little changed. A region of pleasant, wood-covered hills, it was devoted to farming and to large estates maintained by wealthy New Yorkers. Its fresh, untainted air was considered healthful; Edgar Allan Poe brought his wife to Fordham, in the Bronx, hoping that she would benefit from the change in climate.

It was only from the middle 1800's on that spurts in population began to be felt in the borough. From 1850 to 1860, population nearly tripled, and with increasing loads of Irish, Germans, Italians and Jews of Russian and Polish extraction, the Bronx rapidly climbed to its present status of third most populous borough, with 1,394,711 inhabitants.

Sectionally, the Bronx breaks into West, Middle and East. Each of these is essentially a residential area. In the West Bronx, most densely peopled of the three regions, upper middle class residents occupy the more modern skyscraper apartments. In this section are the Grand Concourse, show street of the borough; Van Cortlandt Park, Riverdale, a suburban district; Yankee Stadium, home of the New York Yankees; four of the colleges and universities which give the Bronx its classification as "Borough of Universities," and the huge Bronx Terminal Market—receiving point of much of the city's fruits and vegetables. Through the Middle Bronx are scattered industrial areas, poverty-ridden slums and tiny, far-flung suburbs; Bronx Park (see pp. 320-329) and Woodlawn, with its well-known cemetery. Eastern Bronx somewhat resembles New England coastal areas in the tiny settlements that dot Westchester and Pugsley's Creeks, Eastchester Bay and Baxter Creek Inlet. The Pelham Bay Park area, which contains the greatest population concentration of the section, also includes the Triborough Bridge, the Bronx-Whitestone Bridge, Orchard Beach, City Island, where luxury sailboat building flourishes, and Potter's Field on Hart's Island.

The parks of the Bronx, Yankee Stadium and preserved historic landmarks bring most outsiders to the borough. Its connecting bridges and highways running north to New England and south to the remainder of New York City lead many quickly through it. Boston Post Road, Saw Mill River Parkway and the Bronx River Parkway are heavily traveled roads; the Bronx-Whitestone and Triborough assist 12 other bridges; three subway lines link the borough with Manhattan.

Yet from whatever angle the Bronx is examined, it retains its essentially residential quality.

Grass-planted islands (above) dot side streets leading to the Grand Concourse, site of the finest apartment houses in the Bronx.

The Woodlawn-Jerome subway line (center) is elevated where it

passes the Yankee Stadium in New York's Bronx.

Famous Bronx landmarks are the Poe Cottage, Kingsbridge Road and the Concourse, where *Annabel Lee* and *Ulalume* were written . . .

. . . Van Cortlandt House, in Van Cortlandt Park, near the Broadway and 242nd St. entrance, which now houses a Colonial Museum . . .

... and the ten-storied, neo-classic Bronx County Building (above), containing courtrooms and offices for borough officials.

The Bronx Center of Hunter College (above), at Bedford Park Boulevard and Paul Avenue, is a division of the largest municipally operated woman's college in the world. It achieved international fame by housing first sessions of the UN Security Council in 1946.

Adding to the Bronx's reputation as "Borough of Universities" are New York University, whose outdoor Hall of Fame is seen above . . .

. . . and Fordham University, one of America's largest Catholic educational institutions. Manhattan College is nearby.

Bronx Park

A VISIT at Bronx Park, half an hour by subway from Times Square, is one of New York's favorite trips to the country. Situated in the Bronx, the park's 700 woodland acres provide a refuge of natural beauty. The Bronx River, winding through a valley 15 miles long, feeds two lakes. There are many pleasant paths to follow and quiet places in which to eat a picnic lunch. Nature lovers may visit the world-famed New York Zoological Park, largest in America, and the New York Botanical Garden, both located within the park.

Yearly some three million people visit New York Zoological Park, popularly called the Bronx Zoo. Tractor trains with gay awnings take visitors from Boston Road Gate, southwest entrance, to the main exhibits near Fountain Parking Circle at the north end. The Zoo has 30 permanent buildings, numerous animal ranges and outdoor cages displaying 2,600 mammals, birds and reptiles. At the Zoo are the Question House, where attendants answer queries on animal life, the Primate House, Farm-in-the-Zoo, Bear Dens and five restaurants, including the Zoobar and Flamingo Terrace.

The 230 acres of the New York Botanical Garden (pp. 326-329) lie north of the Zoo, separated from it by Pelham Parkway. The Garden is a year round flower show with an outstanding collection of 12,000 different kinds of plants. It has an herbarium of two million pressed plants and a horticultural library of 51,000 volumes. Of particular interest are the five-acre Wild Flower, Meadow and Rock Garden containing 2,000 varieties; and the Rose Garden of 700 species.

The bronze Rainey Gate, on Pelham Parkway, is the Concourse entrance to the Bronx Zoo. A tree-lined driveway leads to a parking lot.

Animals and birds wander freely in the veldt setting of the African Plains, opened in 1940. Here are several kinds of antelopes . . .

. . . and cranes, ostriches and storks. Lions (above) live on Lion Island, separated by moats from less dangerous animals.

The Zoo has many attractions for the young. Ten cents buys a ride on a camel, llama or pony in an enclosure near Elephant House.

The Children's Zoo, with pint-size exhibits, admits adults only if escorted by children. A grown-up stoops under entrance (above).

Inside is a play ring where children pet ducks and lambs, as well as a Noah's Ark (above), a Wishing Seat, a Baa-Baa Black Sheep.

The Botanical Garden outdoor beds bloom from spring to late fall.

Daffodils (above) flower on slopes and meadows in April and May.

Lotus Flowers of East India decorate one of two waterlily pools
in the court of the Garden's conservatories. Of the fifteen green
houses, one is given over to geraniums, another to a collection of
fibrous-rooted begonias, a third to a Tropical Rain Forest.

328

Among the 750 kinds of orchids in the conservatories are *On-cidium Cavendishinum* (left) and *Cattleya Lida Alba* (right) . . .

. . . a single spray orchid (left) and *Cymbidium* (right). Other indoor displays include 1,500 desert plants, tropical ferns and palms.

Queens

ANY HOUSING SHORTAGE that exists in the Borough of Queens is not for lack of available land on which to build. Sprawling across 121 square miles of the western tip of Long Island, Queens is the largest of New York City's five boroughs in area, but its most undeveloped.

Although Queens is separated from the Bronx and Manhattan by the East River, it is across Newtown Creek, partial boundary between Queens and Brooklyn, that most of its industrial shipments are made. The tonnage which passes over this body of water is greater, by some estimates, than that of the Mississippi River. However, outside of Long Island City, into which most of Queens' industrial plants are crowded, the borough is almost completely residential.

The borough is composed of a string of separate communities, some dating back to pre-Revolution days, others thrown up within recent years. This juxtaposition of old and new gives to Queens' landscape a varied appearance, sometimes unattractive, sometimes charming. One community may be entirely fashioned of modern, spacious garden apartments; the next may preserve a small-town idea of one- and two-family dwellings. New developments spring up so rapidly in Queens that eventually, if and when a saturation point is reached, the borough will resemble a patch-quilt of communities blending every type of architecture into one consolidated mass.

Regionally, the borough breaks into North, Middle and South Queens. Five bays carve the North Shore into a series of peninsulas. East from Flushing small suburbs merge with wealthy neighboring residential areas in Nassau County; to the west, the North Shore, from Flushing to Astoria, is a compact, fully developed region of multiple and single family dwellings. From Astoria, the Triborough Bridge connects Queens with the Bronx and Manhattan; from Whitestone, another separate community in North Queens, the Bronx-Whitestone Bridge crosses the East River. Other districts in this section are Jackson Heights, Corona, Flushing and Little Neck. Flushing Meadow Park, site of the New York World's Fair, is one of the largest municipal parks in the city.

Middle Queens possesses a little of everything that is Queens. At Long Island City are the important industrial plants of the borough; in Maspeth and Ridgewood, its cemeteries; from Jackson Heights to Kew Gardens, its greatest concentration of "garden homes"; and at Jamaica is the Long Island Railroad's transfer point to all parts of the island. At Long Island City is the Queens anchor of the Queensboro Bridge to Manhattan's 59th Street, and the borough's half of the Queens' Midtown Tunnel.

With its string of beaches and two of the most famous racetracks in the country, South Queens is a playground for the remainder of New York City. Ozone Park, Howard Beach and the Rockaways are the more popular resorts. Racing was first introduced to Long Island in 1665 by the British and has flourished there ever since. Today, at Jamaica and Aqueduct, huge throngs congregate during the racing seasons (see Calendar of Events in *Appendix*).

At one time, Queens was available only to those who possessed automobiles, but since the coming of the subways and the Long Island Railroad, her beaches, race tracks and over 100 parks and playgrounds are readily accessible. In addition, bridge and tunnel links with the remainder of the city carry vehicular traffic across miles of fine boulevards and highways in Queens to outlying points on Long Island.

Towering over a swimming pool (above), Hell Gate Bridge makes possible direct rail linkage of New England, the West and South.

Developed as a low-cost, government-financed housing project, the Queensbridge Houses (above) contain 26 six-story elevator units.

333

As many as 50,000 people will pack the stands at Belmont Park on a

single racing day. Entrance to the park is at Queens Village.

The Congregational Church (above) is in Flushing, where early settlers waged bitter battles over issues of religious tolerance.

Built in 1661, the Bowne House (above) was the Flushing meeting place for the Society of Friends. William Penn visited it in 1770.

Scene of national professional and Davis Cup matches are the courts of the West Side Tennis Club at Forest Hills, Queens.

Remnant of the World's Fair of 1939-40 is the New York City Building, renowned as a 1946 seat of the UN General Assembly.

As recently as 1914, Jackson Heights was referred to as "the corn-fields of Queens." Today, however, the only community outside of Manhattan served by the Fifth Avenue bus line, it has developed into a community of "garden apartments," playgrounds and parks.

Jones Beach

CONVERTING a sandbar off the south shore of Long Island into 2,400-acre Jones Beach State Park required one of the greatest dredging operations ever attempted in this country. Originally, the highest point on the sand bar was two feet above sea level, but by scooping 40,000,000 cubic yards of sand from the reef's inland bay and placing it down the mid-line of the proposed park area, altitude was raised to 14 feet.

Jones Beach, opened in 1929, is connected with New York City, 33 miles away, by several super highways which annually carry over 4,000,000 people to the playground. The complete recreational plant includes two bathhouses, one of which can accommodate 10,000 bathers, a heated swimming pool, a 78-acre parking lot, a boardwalk along which archery, deck tennis and shuffleboard can be played, a soft-ball diamond, golf course, Indian Village for children, kindergartens, calisthenics and swimming classes, band concerts, water shows and fireworks. The boardwalk stretches for a mile and is decorated in nautical fashion; for example, drinking fountains are concealed in binnacles.

Every effort has been made to keep the beach clean; more trash cans per square foot dot the sands of Jones Beach than at any other seaside resort. Decorum is maintained by strict enforcement of such rules as "No undressing in cars," "No over-affectionate displays." Men in undershirts are tactfully reprimanded. In fact, so impressive is the entire establishment that after a visit, H. G. Wells, late British author, wrote, "It is one of the finest beaches in the United States, and almost the only one designed with forethought and good taste."

Focal point of Jones Beach is the Central Mall, overshadowed by a
water tower (above) visible 25 miles away. On either side of the

water tower are paved parking lots; fronting the boardwalk (left to right) are a Music Shell for dancing, a cafeteria and a cafe.

Without side shows, roller coasters and games of chance, Jones Beach provides wholesome outdoor fun. Roller skating (above) . . .

. . . pitch-and-putt golf and soft-ball facilities flank the board-walk. The soft-ball field (above) is illuminated for night games.

Facing Zachs Bay is a spacious marine stadium, always packed to capacity during regularly scheduled fireworks displays (above).

Other Points of Interest

AQUEDUCT RACE TRACK—One of two race tracks located within Queens County, Aqueduct is also known as Queens County Jockey Club. Its mile and a quarter course contains the longest homestretch of any track in America—770 yards. (See Calendar of Annual Events for racing dates.)

CHURCH OF THE HOLY TRINITY—Minard Lefever, designer of many of Brooklyn's most beautiful churches, was responsible for the architecture of the Church of the Holy Trinity (Protestant Episcopal), considered one of his best efforts. The church, built in 1847, stands at the corner of Clinton and Montague streets and is of Gothic design.

CROTONA PARK—A small park area at Prospect and Crotona avenues in the Bronx was at one time the estate of the second Gouverneur Morris and on another occasion the Bathgate farm. At present it contains a large swimming pool and a tiny artificial lake used for boating and skating.

DITMAS HOMESTEAD—A Dutch Colonial farmhouse, built by a branch of one of Brooklyn's oldest families, now houses the Faculty Club of Brooklyn College. Prior to the Revolution, a race track occupied the site of the farm.

FORT TOTTEN—Overlooking the junction of the East River, Long Island Sound and Little Neck Bay is this fort in Queens, long important in the New York harbor's defense system. A military installation since 1862, it was converted to a coast artillery fort in 1901.

GEOGRAPHICAL CENTER OF NEW YORK CITY—Collectors of incidental intelligence will be interested to learn that the geographic center of the city lies 200 feet west of Reid Avenue, between Van Buren St. and Greene Ave. in Brooklyn.

JACOB RAPALYE HOUSE—Built in 1749, this house, on Shore Blvd., Queens, is now owned and used by the Consolidated Edison Co. Beautifully preserved, it overlooks Hell Gate Channel.

JAMAICA RACE TRACK—Queens' second track is Jamaica, otherwise known as the Metropolitan Jockey Club. Used exclusively for flat racing, it has no steeplechase course.

KINGS COUNTY HOSPITAL—One of the largest municipal hospitals in the United States is on Clarkson Ave., Brooklyn. Kings County Hospital, established in 1831, has the greatest bed capacity in the city—2,825—and over 500 leading city physicians, who serve without pay, comprise the visiting staff.

KISSENA PARK—A golf course, tennis courts, ball fields and a lake make 219-acre Kissena Park a playground for the North Queens area.

MANHATTAN COLLEGE—One of the schools contributing to the Bronx's reputation as "borough of universities" is Manhattan College, at 242nd Street. Supervised by the Catholic Order of the Brothers of the Christian Schools, the college offers training in science, engineering and business.

MINEOLA, LONG ISLAND—About 18 miles out on the island from Queensboro Bridge is Mineola, best known for its annual county fair sponsored by the Queens-Nassau Agricultural Society.

NEW YORK STATE MERCHANT MARINE ACADEMY—Called the Annapolis of the American Merchant Marine, the academy at Fort Schuyler in the Bronx trains youths between 17 and 21 years.

ONDERDONK FARMHOUSE—A group of Colonial structures, their white fences and cobbled walks still intact, nestle among the factories in the Newtown Creek section of Queens.

Best preserved is the Onderdonk Farmhouse, a two-story stone dwelling, built in 1731.

PELHAM BAY PARK—Largest park in the city, Pelham, in the northeastern section of the Bronx, contains 1,997 acres embracing Twin Island, Orchard Beach, Hunter's Island and Rodman's Neck. Golfing on two 18-hole courses and bathing in Long Island Sound are the big attractions.

PETER RAPALYE HOUSE—Eighteenth-century Long Island farmers stopped for refreshments at the bar of the Peter Rapalye House in Queens, before continuing on to Manhattan with their produce. Both this house and the old Manhattan Club on Madison Ave. claim the distinction of concocting the first Manhattan cocktail.

QUEENS COLLEGE—One of New York's four municipal colleges is Queens College, on Kissena Blvd. Opened in 1937, the school plant consists of nine buildings of Spanish Mission architecture.

RUSSIAN GREEK ORTHODOX CHURCH OF THE TRANSFIGURATION OF OUR LORD—Oriental towers cap the Byzantine-styled Russian Greek church at N. 12th St. and Driggs Ave., Brooklyn. Its congregation is composed of Russian residents of Greenpoint and Williamsburg.

SAILORS' SNUG HARBOR—Ever since 1833 Sailors' Snug Harbor has been taking care of indigent American seamen who have reached the age of 65. Overlooking the Kill Van Kull on Staten Island, the home provides the men with everything from tobacco to movies under a private endowment.

ST. ANN'S CHURCH—Known as "the mother of Brooklyn churches" because its members helped organize St. Mary's, St. Luke's, two St. Paul's, St. John's and Christ Church, St. Ann's (Protestant Episcopal), which now stands at 131 Clinton St., held its first services at 40 Fulton St. in 1784.

ST. RAYMOND'S CEMETERY—Near the Whittemore Street entrance of St. Raymond's Cemetery in the Bronx, "Jafsie" Condon paid $50,000 to Bruno Richard Hauptmann, convicted kidnaper of Charles A. Lindbergh's child, as ransom in a vain effort to return the child safely.

SAYVILLE, LONG ISLAND—Packing headquarters for Blue Point oysters, Sayville, 51 miles from the Manhattan Bridge on Great South Bay, is also a famous yachting center containing one of the finest courses on the bay. A ferry connects Sayville with Fire Island, noted summer resort.

THEODORE ROOSEVELT HOME AND GRAVE — Although most people think of Oyster Bay as Theodore Roosevelt's home, the house is actually located in neighboring Cove Neck. The former president's grave lies nearby, in an area containing Roosevelt Bird Sanctuary and Roosevelt Memorial Park. Roosevelt's home is opened to Boy Scouts only, one day a year.

UNDERWOOD MANSION—On the lawn of the Underwood Mansion, family residence of the late typewriter king, is the Graham Old Ladies' Home, on Washington Ave., Brooklyn.

VAN CORTLANDT PARK—A variety of winter and summer recreational facilities is contained in the 1,132 acres of Van Cortlandt Park in the Bronx. Among its attractions are roller skating rinks, tennis courts, two 18-hole golf links, baseball diamonds, hiking trails, ski hills, hockey fields, bridle paths, horseshoe pitching courts and a 36-acre lake for boating and skating.

WALT WHITMAN PLAQUE—On the southwest corner of Cranberry and Fulton Streets, Brooklyn, is a bronze tablet marking the site of the print shop in which Whitman's "Leaves of Grass" was type-set in 1855. Whitman edited *The Brooklyn Eagle* for two years before the Civil War.

The windswept peninsula of the Rockaways stretches along South

Queens to enclose Jamaica Bay and provide beaches and homes.

The Village of Cutchogue, close to Long Island Sound, has restored
The Old House (above), built in 1649, and opened it to the public.
The interior is designed around the central fireplace. Other early
details are its Colonial furnishings and small window panes.

Caroline Church, named for the English queen, is at Setauket, L.I.

Poet William Cullen Bryant worked in this grist mill, now a museum, at Roslyn, 24 miles from Manhattan on Long Island Sound.

The Hewlett House at Far Rockaway is typical of the dwellings built here in the nineties by New York's fashionable people.

This salt box house is one of many similar dwellings in and near East Setauket, whose fine estates overlook Long Island Sound.

Revolutionary War notables dined at this tavern in Roslyn and visited the mill (upper left, opposite page) on Hempstead Harbor.

Montauk Point Light (background), on the precipitous cliff above
the Atlantic Ocean, marks the eastern extremity of Long Island.

An old mill at East Hampton overlooks an ancient burying ground.

The country around Locust Valley, L.I., is noted for good horses.

West of the Hudson and overlooking Manhattan, Palisades Amusement Park has one of the country's largest roller-coasters.

Tall marsh grass of the Jersey Meadows rises from the tidal swamp alongside several of the highways which lead to New York City.

Visitors to New York may catch this final panorama of Manhattan, with Jersey City's piers and the Hudson in the foreground.

Appendix

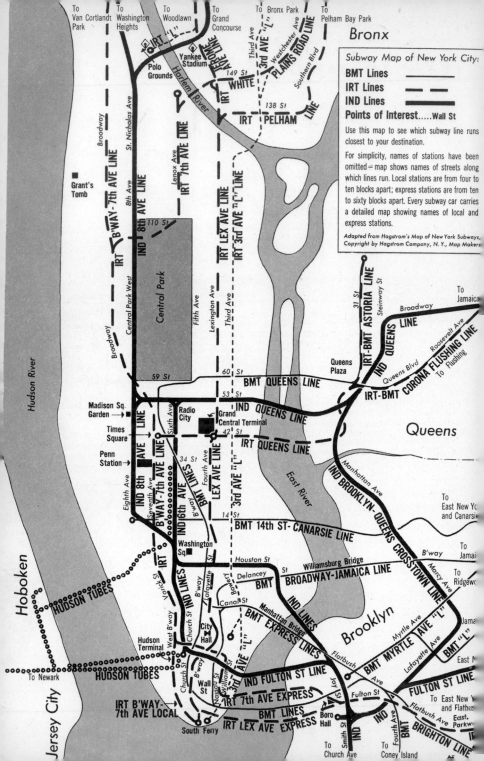

Subway Map of New York City:

BMT Lines ————————

IRT Lines – – – – – – –

IND Lines — — — — —

Points of Interest.....Wall St

Use this map to see which subway line runs closest to your destination.

For simplicity, names of stations have been omitted — map shows names of streets along which lines run. Local stations are from four to ten blocks apart; express stations are from ten to sixty blocks apart. Every subway car carries a detailed map showing names of local and express stations.

Adapted from Hagstrom's Map of New York Subways, Copyright by Hagstrom Company, N. Y., Map Makers

Bronx

Queens

Brooklyn

Hoboken

Jersey City

To Van Cortlandt Park

To Washington Heights

To Woodlawn

To Grand Concourse

To Bronx Park

To Pelham Bay Park

To Jamaica

To Flushing

To East New York and Canarsie

To Jamai

To Ridgewood

Jama

East N

To East New York and Flatbush

East.

To Church Ave

To Coney Island

To Newark

Broadway

St. Nicholas Ave

Harlem River

Yankee Stadium

Polo Grounds

Grant's Tomb

Central Park West

Central Park

Fifth Ave

Lexington Ave

Third Ave

Lenox Ave

8th Ave

110 St

149 St

138 St

IRT WHITE

IRT PELHAM LINE

PLAINS ROAD LINE

Westchester Ave

Southern Blvd

Third Ave

3rd AVE "L"

JEROME AVE LINE

IRT "L"

IRT

B'WAY- 7TH AVE LINE

IND 8TH AVE LINE

IRT 7TH AVE LINE

IRT LEX AVE LINE

IRT 3rd AVE "L" LINE

59 St

60 St

53 St

42 St

34 St

14 St

31 St

Steinway St

Roosevelt Ave

Broadway

IRT-BMT ASTORIA LINE

IND QUEENS LINE

IRT-BMT CORONA FLUSHING LINE

Queens Blvd

Queens Plaza

BMT QUEENS LINE

IND QUEENS LINE

IRT QUEENS LINE

East River

Manhattan Ave

IND BROOKLYN-QUEENS CROSSTOWN LINE

Madison Sq. Garden

Radio City

Grand Central Terminal

Times Square

Penn Station

Eighth Ave

Seventh Ave

Sixth Ave

Fifth Ave

Fourth Ave

IND 8th AVE LINE

B'WAY-7TH AVE LINE

IND 6th AVE LINES

BMT LINES

LEX AVE LINE

3rd AVE "L"

Hudson River

HUDSON TUBES

HUDSON TUBES

Hudson Terminal

Washington Sq

Houston St

Varick St

West B'way

Church St

B'way

Lafayette St

Bowery

Canal St

Manhattan Bridge

IND LINES

IRT

City Hall

Wall St

Nassau St

William St

3rd AVE "L"

IND FULTON ST LINE

IRT 7th AVE EXPRESS

BMT LINES

IRT LEX AVE EXPRESS

IRT B'WAY- 7TH AVE LOCAL

South Ferry

Boro Hall

Smith St

Jay St

Fulton St

Flatbush Ave

Fourth Ave

IND

BMT

BRIGHTON LINE

Delancey St

Williamsburg Bridge

BROADWAY-JAMAICA LINE

BMT

BMT 14th ST-CANARSIE LINE

BMT EXPRESS LINES

Myrtle Ave

Lafayette Ave

Marcy Ave

BMT MYRTLE AVE "L"

BMT "L"

East

FULTON ST LINE

Flatbush Ave

East. Parkwy

B'way

TRANSPORTATION

APPROACHING THE EARTH through separating layers of stratosphere and atmosphere, a visitor from another planet would be aware of New York City even before it came into view. His sensitive equipment would register, with earthquake-like violence, the ceaseless humming, screeching, and clacking of the most complex transportation system ever devised.

While New York City was becoming the recognized business, shipping, cultural and tourist center of the nation, a gigantic problem in logistics developed. Stated simply, the question was one of permitting 80,000,000 annual visitors, business and pleasure bent, and a million daily commuters, to find entrance to the metropolitan area; then, after arrival, to find means of their sharing with metropolitan dwellers already overtaxed intra-city transportation facilities.

Taking 1945 as a sample year, here is how this was accomplished. Of more than 80,000,000 arrivals, over 70,000,000 came by rail; 9,000,000 by automobile; 2,000,000 by air; one and a half million by bus; and the remainder by ship. Actually, there was more to it than that. For instance, of the total number arriving by rail, 54 per cent came through Pennsylvania Station; 22 per cent through Grand Central Terminal; 14 per cent through the Long Island Railroad in Pennsylvania Station; 6 per cent through Jersey City; 3 per cent through Hoboken; and one per cent through Weehawken. Of the 9,000,000 incoming motorists, 42 per cent drove through the Holland and Lincoln tunnels from New Jersey; 25 per cent over the George Washington Bridge from New Jersey; 18 per cent across the Boston Post Road and Merritt Parkway from New England; 8 per cent on Hudson River ferries from New Jersey; and another 8 per cent across the Henry Hudson Parkway from Northern New York.

Once planted in New York City, the visitor has at his disposal a transportation set-up of subways, elevated railways, buses and trolleys which embraces a total route mileage of 554 miles and 1,237 miles of tracks—enough to connect New York with Chicago. Awesome when contemplated by uninitiated out-of-towners, taken for granted by blasé Gothamites, this criss-crossing of artery-like travel lines represents the ties that bind together and make accessible the far-flung portions of New York City's five boroughs.

Best known of the many means of transportation available in New York City are its subways. Municipally-owned, they are the largest, most used and most expensive construction of their kind in the world. Each year, over two billion passengers jam into one of the three operating divisions, paying out $125,000,000 in fares, a nickel at a time. Although it is possible to ride the subways forever without payment of additional fare (by simply remaining on a train which retraces its route), the longest ride in one direction, without a change, is a 26.13-mile run from East 241st Street and White Plains Road, the Bronx, to New Lots Avenue, Brooklyn.

So much a part of a New Yorker's daily speech are the abbreviations of the three main subway lines that few people, if asked, could correctly identify their official titles. IRT, BMT and IND stand for Interborough Rapid Transit, Brooklyn-Manhattan Transit and City Subway System, the last-named more commonly known as the Independent Subway.

Each line is further sub-divided into categories designed to give passengers an inkling of the trains' eventual destinations. The IRT breaks down into two main divisions, West Side Line (Broadway-7th Avenue) and East Side Line (Lexington-4th Avenue). The Broadway-7th Avenue Line runs between New Lots Avenue, Brooklyn, and 242nd Street (Van Cortlandt Park), the Bronx. However, a trunk line of this Division cuts over from 96th Street, Manhattan, to Bronx Park. The Lexington-4th Avenue Line runs from Utica Avenue, Brooklyn, to Woodlawn Cemetery and to 241st St. and White Plains Rd. in the Bronx, with branches to Pelham Bay Park and to Dyre Ave. In addition, there is service from Times Square to both Astoria and Flushing in Queens, and a shuttle from Times Square to Grand Central.

The BMT is essentially a Brooklyn line, crossing into Manhattan only as far as 60th Street. Its main purpose is to connect the sprawling Borough of Brooklyn with mid- and downtown Manhattan. Its main divisions are the Brighton Beach, Sea Beach and West End Lines, which run to Stillwell Avenue in Coney Island. The Culver Line terminates at West 8th Street in Coney Island, and the 4th Avenue Line at 95th Street in Brooklyn's Bay Ridge section. Other branches of the BMT head for Queensboro Plaza and 168th St. (Jamaica), both in Queens, and to Rockaway Parkway (end of the 14th St.-Canarsie Line). A branch of the BMT-Jamaica line terminates at Metropolitan Ave. in Ridgewood (Queens).

Newest additions to the metropolitan subways are the 6th and 8th Ave. trunks of the IND, whose first trains began operation in 1932, and whose trackage has been constantly added to. The 8th Ave. Line serves Manhattan, Queens, Brooklyn and the Bronx, with trains running from 205th St. in the Bronx, Jamaica in Queens, and 207th St. in Manhattan, through the Borough of Manhattan, to the Fulton St. line and to Church Ave. in Brooklyn. The 6th Ave. Line carries IND passengers on a parallel route through the center of Manhattan between 53rd and W. 4th Streets with a branch running through the Lower East Side. (See subway map, page 362.)

In addition to subways, New York's boroughs are welded together by bus, trolley and the few remaining elevated lines. (Most of the elevated lines have been removed and are being replaced by subways. Trolleys similarly have been disappearing, leaving the prospect for the future of a completely bus-and-subway-served city.) Manhattan's bus lines run up every avenue from 1st to 10th, and cross the borough at such main cross streets as 14th, 34th, 42nd, 50th, 59th, 72nd and 96th. For complete details concerning bus and trolley lines in each borough consult street guides to New York City, available at all newsstands.

Despite New York's traffic burden, motorists find its parkway system, traffic light system and clearly defined "one-way" streets and "no parking" streets designed to facilitate quick entry to and exit from the city. Separable from the parkways mentioned above, which lead into the city, there are some superb examples of highway engineering within the city itself. Manhattan's circumferential East and West Side drives will permit a complete drive around the borough without once stopping for red lights, cross traffic or other obstacles to pleasant driving. Out on Long Island, roads such as Grand Central Parkway and Southern Parkway are designed to eliminate as much cross traffic as possible by use of cloverleafs and under and over passes.

Probably the most maligned means of transportation in the city is its taxicabs. Whenever two or more New York visitors meet, sooner or later their conversation veers around to the seemingly mad antics of the city's hackies. Despite their dare-devil stunts, cab drivers are, by insurance statistics, among the safest group of motorists in the country. They know the city thoroughly and are usually among the friendliest and most helpful people a visitor will meet.

From its Saw Mill River Parkway connection at the Westchester County line, the Henry Hudson Parkway cuts across the West . . .

. . . Bronx and then flows into the West Side (Miller) Highway at a point several blocks below the graceful 79th St. cloverleaf (above).

Carrying 24 per cent of the city's vehicular traffic from New Jersey is the 4,760-foot, Hudson-spanning George Washington Bridge.

Many visitors arriving in New York by air come through La Guardia Field (above), where up to 600 planes have been handled in a day.

Jersey motorists heading for mid-Manhattan utilize Lincoln Tunnel (above), whose two tubular roadways lie beneath the Hudson River.

From Long Island and points west and south, over 35,000,000 visitors enter the city annually through Pennsylvania Station (above).

Midtown skyscrapers tower over the three blocks occupied by Grand Central Terminal (above), New York's other great railroad station.

The 17,710-foot, over-all elevated spans of the Triborough Bridge

provide easy automobile access to Manhattan, Queens and the Bronx.

Most recently built, most comfortable and cleanest of New York's subways are 6th and 8th Avenue Lines of the Independent System.

During rush hours, the West Shore Ferry (above), which runs from 42nd Street to Weehawken, New Jersey, is stampeded by commuters.

Gothamites eye the Third Avenue "El" (above) wistfully. One of
New York's few remaining overhead railways, it, too, will soon go.

NEW YORK CITY possesses the greatest concentration of recreational facilities in the world. Below is a list of New York's major attractions. For more specific information as to time, price and, in some instances, exact location, consult the Police Department Information Booth, Broadway and 43rd St.; the Travelers Aid Society at both Grand Central Terminal and Pennsylvania Station; the American Automobile Association, 28 East 78th St.; or the classified telephone directory.

Theaters

Although each community in the five boroughs is sprinkled with motion picture houses, the theater district is commonly known as the area from 42nd St. north to 59th St., between Sixth and Eighth avenues, in Manhattan. Here are most of the legitimate theaters and the larger motion picture houses. At night, with its million light bulbs blazing, this Times Square section forms the "Great White Way."

Restaurants

Whether you wish plain American cooking or exotic concoctions from countries over the world, there is a restaurant in New York City to satisfy. From self-service cafeterias and "nickel-in-the-slot" Automats to Park Avenue swank, a dining room is available to fit any budget or appetite. Consult the classified telephone directory, or the magazines *New Yorker* and *Cue,* for complete listings.

Night Clubs

With the exception of Greenwich Village and Harlem, New York's theater district houses nearly all of the city's night clubs. Entertainment found at various spots runs from quiet, dignified piano interludes to brassy, flashy floor shows. Both *Cue* and the *New Yorker* will indicate type of entertainment and minimum or cover charges. It is advisable to telephone for reservations.

Music

Music lovers will find New York's offerings the most varied in the country. Indoor concerts and recitals are given at the following places: Brooklyn Academy of Music, Lafayette Ave. and Ashland Pl., Brooklyn; Brooklyn Museum, Eastern Parkway and Washington Ave.; Carnegie Hall, 7th Ave. and 57th St.; McMillin Academic Theatre, Columbia University, Broadway and 116th St.; Metropolitan Museum of Art, 5th Ave. and 82nd St.; Steinway Concert Hall, 113 W. 57th St.; Town Hall, 123

W. 43rd St.; Washington Irving High School, Irving Place and 16th St. Outdoor concerts and recitals in summer may be heard at Central Park Mall; Lewisohn Stadium, Amsterdam Ave. and 138th St.; Prospect Park, Brooklyn. Major operatic performances are given at the Metropolitan Opera House, Broadway and 39th St. (pp. 162-169). For dates of concerts telephone individual establishments or consult newspapers.

Spectator Sports

Indoor sporting center of the city is Madison Square Garden (pp. 210-217) while smaller arenas are scattered throughout the boroughs: Randall's Island Stadium, in the East River; Columbia University's Baker Field, 218th St. and Broadway; City College's Lewisohn Stadium; New York University's Ohio Field, 181st St. and University Ave. Listed below are other sites of New York's outdoor sporting activities.

BASEBALL PARKS—Ebbets Field, Brooklyn, Bedford Ave. and Sullivan Place (Dodgers); Polo Grounds, 8th Ave. and 155th St. (N.Y. Giants); Yankee Stadium, River Ave. and 161st St. (N.Y. Yankees).

RACE TRACKS—Aqueduct, Aqueduct, Queens; Belmont Park, Belmont Park, Long Island; Empire City, Yonkers, New York; Jamaica, Jamaica, Queens.

Boat Trips

Boat trips operate in waters surrounding the city during summer months. The following excursions are offered: *Atlantic Highlands and North Jersey Shore; Hudson River,* leaving from W. 42nd St. piers; *Long Island Sound* and *Coney Island,* leaving from Battery.

Trips may be taken around Manhattan Island and to Governors and Bedloe Islands. The Staten Island Ferry leaves from South Street.

Amusement Parks

During the summer nationally-known amusement parks operate. In and around the city are Palisades Amusement Park, Palisades, N.J., opposite W. 125th St.; Playland, at Rye Beach, New York; Rockaways' Playland at Rockaway Beach, Queens; and Steeplechase Park, Coney Island, Brooklyn.

Sight-seeing

BUS AND LIMOUSINE TOURS—See classified directory under "sight-seeing" for addresses of companies providing tours of points of interest in city.

STUDY GROUP TOURS—Reconciliation Trips, 417 W. 121st St.; Sloane House (Y.M.C.A.) Tours, 356 W. 34th St.

OBSERVATION TOWERS—Bank of Manhattan Co. Bldg., 40 Wall St., 71st floor; Chanin Bldg., 122 E. 42nd St., 54th floor; Chrysler Bldg.. 405 Lexington Ave., 71st floor; Empire State Bldg., 350 5th Ave., 86th and 102nd floors; RCA Bldg., 30 Rockefeller Plaza, 70th floor; Sixty Wall Tower, 70 Pine St., 66th floor; Woolworth Bldg., 233 Broadway. 60th floor.

FLIGHTS OVER CITY—Sightseeing plane flights are available at the following bases, arrangements for flights can be made by telephone: Staten Island Airport, Greenridge, Richmond; Richmond County Airport, Inc., Travis, Staten Island; Rockaway Airport, Rockaway Beach, Long Island; Mill Basin Seaplane Base, Brooklyn, New York; Seaplane Base, East River, Foot of 154th Place, Whitestone, Long Island; Donovan Hughes Airport, Fresh Kills Bridge, Staten Island; Seaplane Base, College Point, New York; Cater-White Seaplane Base, Inc., foot of Dyckman St., North River; Metropolitan Seaplane Bases, Inc., North River between 156th and 157th streets; Parkway Seaplane Base, foot of Bay 32nd St., Brooklyn, Flushing Airport, Flushing, Queens; Evers Seaplane Base, Bronx, New York; Wall St. Seaplane Base, foot of Wall St. and East River; E. 23rd St. Seaplane Base, foot of 23rd St. and East River.

OCEAN LINERS—When large transatlantic liners are in North River docks, they may be visited. Passes may be had by applying at the pier.

RADIO STUDIOS—Tickets for commercial broadcasts may be secured by applying to sponsors, in care of the broadcasting company; for sustaining programs, apply directly to the broadcasting company; American Broadcasting Co., 30 Rockefeller Plaza; Columbia Broadcasting System, Inc., 485 Madison Ave.; Mutual Broadcasting System, Inc., 1440 Broadway; National Broadcasting Co., 30 Rockefeller Plaza.

Museums

American Academy of Arts and Letters, 633 W. 155th St.; American Geographical Society, Broadway at 156th St.; Brooklyn Botanical Gardens, 1000 Washington Ave., Brooklyn; Brooklyn Museum, Eastern Parkway and Washington Ave., Brooklyn; The Cloisters, Fort Tryon Park (pp. 258-263); Cooper Union Museum for the Arts of Decoration, Cooper Square and 7th St.; Dyckman Home, Broadway and 204th St.; Fraunces Tavern, Broad and Pearl Sts.; Frick Collection, 1 East 70th St.; Hayden Planetarium, Central Park West and 81st St.; Hispanic Society of America, Broadway and 155th St.; Jumel Mansion, Jumel Terrace and West 160th St.; King Mansion, Jamaica Ave. and 153rd St., Jamaica, Queens; Lefferts Homestead, Prospect Park, near entrance at Flatbush and Ocean Aves.; Long Island Historical Society, 130 Pierrepont St., Brooklyn; Masonic Museum, 71 West 23rd St.; Metropolitan Museum of Art, 5th Ave. at 82nd St. (pp. 170-189); Museum of the American Indian, Heye Foundation, Broadway at 155th St.; Museum of the American Numismatic Society, Broadway, between 155th and 156th Sts.; Museum of the City of New York, 5th Ave. at 104th St.; Museum of the Jewish Theological Seminary of America, Broadway and 122nd St.; Museum of Modern Art, 11 West 53rd St.; New York Botanical Gardens and Zoological Park, Bronx Park (pp. 320-329); New–York Historical Society, Central Park West, between 76th and 77th Sts.; New York Museum of Science and Industry, RCA Bldg., Rockefeller Center (pp. 136-147); New York Public Library, 5th Ave. and 42nd St.; Old Merchant's House, 29 East 4th St.; Pierpont Morgan Library, 29 East 36th St.; Poe Cottage, Grand Concourse and Kingsbridge Road, the Bronx; Prospect Park Zoo, Flatbush Ave. near Ocean Ave., Brooklyn; Roosevelt House, 28 East 20th St.; Staten Island Institute of Arts and Sciences, Stuyvesant Pl. and Wall St., St. George, Staten Island; Staten Island Zoological Society, Barrett Park Zoo, West New Brighton, Staten Island; Van Cortlandt House, Van Cortlandt Park, near Broadway and 242nd St. entrance, the Bronx; Whitney Museum of American Art, 10 West 8th St.

Beaches

Atlantic Beach, Long Island; Asbury Park, New Jersey; Brighton Beach, Brooklyn; Coney Island, Brooklyn (pp. 294-301); Jacob Riis Park, Queens; Jones Beach, Wantagh, Long Island (pp. 340-345); Long Beach, Long Island; Long Branch, New Jersey; Manhattan Beach, Brooklyn; Midland Beach, Staten Island; Orchard Beach, Pelham Bay Park, the Bronx; Rockaway Beach, Queens; Rye Beach (Long Island Sound), Rye, N.Y.; South Beach, Staten Island.

Golf

MUNICIPAL COURSES—Clearview, 202-06 Willetts Point Blvd., Queens; Dyker Beach Park, 86th St. and 7th Ave., Brooklyn; Forest Park, Park Lane South and Forest Parkway, Queens; Kissena Park, N. Hempstead Turnpike, Queens; La Tourette Park, Forest Hill Road and London Road, Staten Island; Mosholu, Jerome and Bainbridge Ave., the Bronx; Van Cortlandt Park, 242nd St. and Broadway, the Bronx.

PRIVATE COURSES OPEN TO PUBLIC—Bayside Golf Links, Little Bayside Road, Bayside, Queens; Idlewild Beach Golf Club, Idlewild St., Laurelton, Queens; Mohansic Golf Course, Westchester County Park; Tysen Manor Links, New Dorp Lane and Hylan Blvd., New Dorp, Staten Island.

Swimming Pools

INDOOR—Park Central Hotel, 7th Ave. and 55th St.; St. George Hotel, 51 Clark St., Brooklyn, Shelton Hotel, 525 Lexington Ave.; West Side Y.M.C.A., 5 West 63rd St.

OUTDOOR—Cascades Pool, 134th St. and Broadway; Jerome Cascades, Jerome Ave. and 168th St., the Bronx; Palisades Amusement Park, Palisades, New Jersey; Steeplechase Park, Coney Island, Brooklyn.

MUNICIPAL SWIMMING POOLS—Carmine Street Pool, 83 Carmine St.; Colonial Pool, Broadhurst Ave. and W. 146th St.; East 23rd Street Pool, E. 23rd St. and Ave. A; East 54th Street Pool, 342 E. 54th St.; Hamilton Fish Pool, E. Houston St. and Sheriff St.; Highbridge Pool, Amsterdam Ave. and W. 173rd St.; John Jay Pool, Franklin D. Roosevelt Drive and 78th St.; Thomas Jefferson Pool, 1st Ave. and 112th St.; West 60th Street Pool, 533 W. 59th St.; West 134th Street Pool, 35 W. 134th St.

Horseback Riding

There are bridle paths in Central Park; Prospect Park and Ocean Parkway, Brooklyn; Pelham Bay and Van Cortlandt Parks and Pelham Parkway, the Bronx; Forest and Kissena Parks, Queens; and in various parks and parkways on Long Island and in Westchester County. Riding academies include Aylward Riding Academy, 32 W. 67th St.; Central Park Riding School, 924 7th Ave.; Corrigan Riding Academy, 56 W. 66th St.; Equestrian Club, 31 W. 98th St.

Other Recreation

Additional recreational facilities can best be located by consulting the classified telephone directory under the following headings: Badminton, Bicycling, Billiards, Boating, Bowling, Ice Skating, Roller Skating, Table Tennis and Tennis. For information concerning hunting, fishing and camping, apply to State Park Commission, 80 Centre Street, New York City.

ESPECIALLY FOR CHILDREN

BROOKLYN CHILDREN'S MUSEUM, Brooklyn Ave. and Park Place—Exhibits are arranged on low tables in this museum exclusively for children. Clay modeling, fingerpainting and block printing rooms, stamp, puppet and science clubs are located here. Movies are shown several days each week.

MUSEUM OF THE AMERICAN INDIAN, Heye Foundation, Broadway at 155th St.—North American Indians almost come to life in displays covering every phase of Indian life from clothing to housing.

METROPOLITAN MUSEUM OF ART, 5th Ave. at 82nd St.—Permanent exhibits such as the Egyptian tomb, Greek collection and the Armor Room bring hours of delight to children.

NEW YORK PUBLIC LIBRARY, 5th Ave. and 42nd St.—The Central Children's Room contains children's books from every land and, from time to time, special exhibits with youth-appeal.

CHILDREN'S ZOO, BRONX PARK, East 182nd St., the Bronx—This is a small-scale zoo set in fairy-tale surroundings, with tame animals for children to ride and play with. A Farm-in-the-Zoo houses a collection of farm animals.

Most beaches in and around the city maintain special wading sections, carefully supervised, for children. At two other large city parks, Prospect and Central, zoos, botanical exhibits and playgrounds are available. A check of the N.Y. *Times'* Friday edition, or of the *New Yorker,* will reveal special weekly doings for the young.

LIST OF ANNUAL EVENTS IN NEW YORK CITY

Except where specified, dates on which the following events are held vary from year to year. For definite dates, write to newspapers, sponsoring organizations or halls where events are held.

JANUARY

National Motorboat Show, Grand Central Palace
Hollywood Ice Revue, Madison Square Garden
Patrolmen's Benevolent Association Ball, Madison Square Garden
Firemen's Benevolent Association Ball, Madison Square Garden
Daily News Silver Skates, Madison Square Garden
Chinese New Year Celebration in Chinatown

FEBRUARY

N.Y. Aviation Show, Grand Central Palace
National Sportsmen's Show, Grand Central Palace
Westminster Kennel Club Dog Show, Madison Square Garden
Milrose Track Meet, Madison Square Garden
National A.A.U. Indoor Track Championship Meet, Madison Square Garden
New York Athletic Club Indoor Track Meet, Madison Square Garden

MARCH

St. Patrick's Day Parade, 5th Avenue (March 17)
Golden Gloves Amateur Boxing Tournament of Champions, Madison Square Garden
National Intercollegiate Basketball finals, Madison Square Garden
Intercollegiate AAA Indoor Track Meet, Madison Square Garden
Antique Show, Madison Square Garden
International Flower Show, Grand Central Palace
Spring ballet season, Metropolitan Opera House

APRIL

Floral Displays, Rockefeller Center (changed monthly, April-October)

Easter Decorations and Chorister Concerts, Rockefeller Center

Army Day Parade, 5th Avenue (April 6)

Easter Parade, 5th Avenue

National Homes Show, Grand Central Palace

Jamaica Race Meet opens

Ringling Brothers, Barnum and Bailey Circus, Madison Square Garden

Baseball season opens at Polo Grounds, Yankee Stadium and Ebbets Field

MAY

May Day Labor Parade (May 1)

Metropolitan Colleges Track and Field Meet, Randall's Island

N.Y. *American* Soccer Club matches, Randall's Island (May and June)

Belmont Park Race Meet opens

JUNE

Metropolitan AAU Track and Field Meet, Randall's Island

Aqueduct Race Meet opens

Empire City Race Meet opens

Symphonic concerts (through August), Lewisohn Stadium

JULY

Cricket Games, Randall's Island (July, August, September)

Polo at Meadowbrook, L.I.

AUGUST

Armenian Youth Federation Track and Field Meet, Randall's Island

Band concerts and folk dancing, Mall, Central Park

SEPTEMBER

Harvest Moon Ball, Madison Square Garden
World's Championship Rodeo, Madison Square Garden
National Business Show, Grand Central Palace
Outdoor Art Exhibition, Washington Square
Aqueduct Race Meet opens fall season
Belmont Race Meet opens fall season

OCTOBER

Press Photographers' Exhibition, Rockefeller Center
National Hardware Show, Grand Central Palace
High School football, Randall's Island
Philadelphia Orchestra, Carnegie Hall
N.Y. Philharmonic-Symphonic Orchestra opens season,
    Carnegie Hall
Empire City Race Meet opens fall season
Jamaica Race Meet opens fall season
Fall ballet season, Metropolitan Opera House

NOVEMBER

Basketball season opens, Madison Square Garden
Hockey season opens, Madison Square Garden
Ice Follies, Madison Square Garden
National Horse Show, Madison Square Garden
Boston Symphony Orchestra, Carnegie Hall
National Orchestral Association, Carnegie Hall
National Hotel Exposition, Grand Central Palace
Macy's Thanksgiving Day Balloon Parade, Broadway—
    110th Street to 34th Street
Grand Opera season opens, Metropolitan Opera House

DECEMBER

Christmas Decorations and Chorister Concerts, Rockefeller Center

PICTURE CREDITS

LOOK AT AMERICA: New York City

Designed by Howard Jensen
Maps drawn by R. M. Chapin
Set in Garamond No. 3 by The Composing Room, Inc.
Offset plates by Graphic Arts Corporation of Ohio
Color printed in offset by The Kellogg & Bulkeley Co.
Monotone in photogravure by Photogravure and Color Company

This book was produced by these members of the LOOK Picture Book Division: James Hosking, Ruth Davis, Edmund Motyka, Jane Fishlock, Noah Sarlat, Ellen Wivegg, David Landman and Amy Hodel. Management of Book Division: Harry Shaw, Director; James Hosking, Executive Editor; Charles C. Moffat, Production Manager; John K. Murphy, Jr., Managing Editor (Text); Edmund Motyka, Managing Editor (Pictures).

We wish to express our thanks to the many persons who contributed to the preparation and production of this volume, including Rebecca B. Rankin, editor of New York Advancing; *the Port of New York Authority; the Moran Towing & Transportation Co.; A. G. Hagstrom; and Alfred J. Starger, of the travel bureau of the Automobile Club of New York.*

The Editors of LOOK

INDEX   (Page numbers in *italics* refer to illustrations)